Bird Feet and the Twelve Steps

Cover photograph courtesy of Helga Minderjahn

Bird Feet
and the
Twelve
Steps

A thoughtful seeker
finds Al-Anon recovery

Bruce W. Hasenyager

AshaPress
Plano Texas USA
2017

AshaPress
1400 Earlshire Place
Plano Texas 75075

Copyright © 2017 by Bruce W. Hasenyager
All rights reserved, including the right to reproduce this book or portions thereof in any form whatsoever.

Hard cover ISBN 9798860314160

Paperback ISBN 978-0-9909005-3-5

2 3 4 5 6 7 8 9 10

The Twelve Steps and Twelve Traditions as adapted by Al-Anon with permission of Alcoholics Anonymous Services World, Inc. ("AAWS") are reprinted with permission of Al-Anon and AAWS. AAWS' permission to reprint Al-Anon's Steps and Traditions does not mean that AAWS has reviewed or approved the contents of this publication, or that AAWS necessarily agrees with the views expressed therein. Alcoholics Anonymous is a program of recovery from alcoholism only - use or permissible adaptation of A.A.'s Steps and Traditions in connection with programs and activities which are patterned after A.A., but which address other problems, or in any other non-A.A. context, does not imply otherwise.

Al-Anon's Twelve Steps and Twelve Traditions are copyrighted by Al-Anon Family Group Headquarters, Inc., and reprinted with permission of Al-Anon Family Group Headquarters, Inc. Permission to reprint does not mean that Al-Anon Family Group Headquarters, Inc. has reviewed or approved the contents of this publication, or that Al-Anon Family Group Headquarters, Inc. necessarily agrees with the views expressed herein. Al-Anon is a program of recovery for families and friends of alcoholics—use of this excerpt in any non Al-Anon context does not imply endorsement or affiliation by Al-Anon.

This book is dedicated to the two who sat with me at that first meeting

Contents

Introduction — 1
Who's it for? — 1
A personal experience of Al-Anon recovery — 2
About that other Bird Feet book — 3

One Al-Anon's Story — 5
I need to start with some ugly facts — 5
What it was like — 6
What happened — 11
What it's like now — 13

The Twelve Step Waltz — 15
Step One — 16
Step Two — 20
Step Three — 33

Discovering Myself — 46
Step Four — 46
Step Five — 55

Commitment — 61
Step Six — 62
Step Seven — 76

Getting The Feel Of A New Life — 82
Step Eight — 82
Step Nine — 87

Grooving The Swing   **93**
    Step Eleven   107
    Step Twelve   119
What Now?   **129**
    Understanding   130
    Discernment   130
    Character   130
    Responsibility   131
    Moderation and balance   131
    Reverence and tolerance   132
Appendixes   **133**
    Step Four Guide   134
    Commentary on The Lord's Prayer   139
    St. Francis Peace Prayer   141
    Glossary of Ambiguous Twelve Step Terms   142
References   **144**
Index   **147**
Acknowledgments   **153**

Bird Feet and the Twelve Steps

Introduction

ONCE I WAS INVITED TO TALK ABOUT THE STEPS at a series of Al-Anon meetings. It was scary the first time I stepped up to speak, and I wasn't sure what I would say, but "Let go and let God," so I started in.

I remember saying that it was my job to speak and theirs to listen, and I said, "I hope I finish before you do." It was good to start with a laugh.

Folks told me it went very well, and they thanked me for what I said. They may have just been trying to be nice, but I'm going to take them at their word and conclude that I have something worthwhile to say on this topic. That's the reason for this book. I'm writing in the same voice I would use if you invited me to be a Step speaker at your meeting. This book lays out in a straightforward way how one damaged, codependent guy learned to understand the Steps, the program, and the miracle.

Who's it for?

Is this the right book for you? Probably, yes. You've picked it up and read this far, suggesting that you have a Twelve Step program, you are considering one, or you want to know more. Maybe you want to have a better program. Perhaps you don't get how a Twelve Step program can help someone who doesn't drink or drug. Perhaps you have a loved one with a problem, and you just want to understand what the Steps are all about. Then, you're in the right place.

The Steps promise a better life. That's the objective. They promise great stuff. If you put the A.A. and Al-Anon promises together, here's what they say we can have:

- *We are promised new* . Courage, delight, love, freedom, and happiness replace uselessness, self-pity, selfishness, shame, resentment, martyrdom, rage, depression, and fear.
- *We are promised new understanding.* We will understand: situations that baffled us; that we are worthy of

love; that we can see reality and truth; that we belong and are worthy; that our fallibility is a feature of our humanity; and that we can benefit others. We will understand that God is doing for us what we cannot do for ourselves, and we will comprehend serenity and know peace.

- *We are promised new actions.* Self-seeking will be gone. We will accept love. We will risk failure to develop our talents. We will be able to provide hope to others. We will stand up for ourselves without opposing others.
- *We will neither forget the past nor regret it.* We will live our lives with ease, balance, and grace. We will laugh more.[1]

These are excellent things; who wouldn't want them? Perhaps you've begun to feel benefits and want more. Maybe you came to the Steps because of a loved one's addictions or compulsions. Maybe the addictions and compulsions were yours. The program leads us into that promised good life, and when we do the Steps and get a better life, our world gets better, and it gets bigger. But, with each new dimension of our better life, we discover that even a good life has struggles, problems, and decisions. We have issues in places where we used not even to have places. So we go back to the Steps for another round.

A personal experience of Al-Anon recovery

If you are a Twelve Step member, you're probably already familiar with the canonical books of the program: Alcoholics Anonymous (the A.A. Big Book), How Al-Anon Works, Courage To Change, and Daily Reflections. You may have already worked with Paths To Recovery and The Twelve Steps and Twelve Traditions. This book covers much of the same territory but goes beyond. There's stuff here you haven't seen before or maybe just haven't thought about this way before.

---

[1] This summary of the promises and many other bits in this book are taken from the daily meditation book Bird Feet In Concrete, a companion to the present volume.

Introduction

Maybe you're curious about the mysteries and ambiguities that abound in the Steps.

Maybe you're curious about how the Steps relate to the whole of spirituality.

Maybe you're interested in the practical details of actually doing the Steps.

Maybe you'd like to know more about sponsorship or service.

Maybe you'd like to think through how emerging cognitive science fits with the practicalities of the Steps.

Or, perhaps you'd just like to see how one person recovered from chaos and confusion to start living the good life that the Steps promise us. No matter what itch of curiosity brought you to pick up this book, you will likely find something here to scratch it.

About that other Bird Feet book

Years ago, I wrote *Bird Feet In Concrete*, a daily meditation book written for experienced Twelve Step women and men who wanted material beyond the usual Twelve Step literature to help them live the good life promised in the Steps. The book's curious title refers to the meditation for February 29th, in which marks on a sidewalk led to a helpful insight about rushing to judgment. It's a good book, and I think it's a big help to the people who use it. I realized, however, that it assumed an awful lot about how readers understood the Twelve Steps and, more important, it assumed they probably understood the Steps and the program more-or-less the same way I do.

People have told me that you can get most of that unique understanding by reading through the daily meditations a few times if you work at it. But, I asked myself, why should I make it so hard? So, I've written this second book. *Bird Feet and the Twelve Steps* carries its funny title so that readers can tell that there is a connection between my recovery experience in Al-Anon, the examination of the Twelve Steps in this book, and the earlier meditation book. Even though each book stands on its own, it probably makes sense to read this one first. The daily meditation book works fine any day of the year whenever you start it.

You'll find bits and pieces of my story scattered throughout the book. I tell the raw stuff so you can get an idea of who I am, a "low bottom Al-Anon." A lot of what happened and what I did on my way down into my pit of despair isn't pretty, but it's my past, my life, and (I eventually discovered) it just isn't all that unusual. In meetings, we find out how much we have in common. I learned I had gone through the same chaos, confusion, pain, and isolation that we all suffer. So now I say we have exactly the same experiences ... in different ways.

My story is mixed in, but the book focuses on my intellectual and spiritual journey through the Twelve Steps, complete with opinions on what the ambiguous parts mean, why the Steps work, and where the Steps have taken me.

The purpose is to give a perspective on the Twelve Steps that adds value to your understanding and your program. There are insights that I found helpful as I went along, and there are ways of understanding things that helped me make sense of what was happening. I'm hoping that the stuff in this book will provoke your thinking, grab your awareness, and, maybe, give you a boost in your recovery. Of course, you may not always agree with my way of thinking about things, and that's just fine. In our Twelve Step program, we can always "take what you want and leave the rest."

So, here we go!

One Al-Anon's Story

THIS CHAPTER WILL GIVE YOU THE BACKGROUND of how I got to where I am. I use the usual pattern for our recovery stories:

- What it was like
- What happened
- What it's like now

I've heard many of these stories. One of the things I have noticed is that because the sometimes wild influence of alcohol on behavior can be so dramatic and extreme, A.A.s usually have a more entertaining story than Al-Anons. A "drunk-a-log" can be hilarious when recited in the past tense by someone in solid recovery. But, on the other hand, our stories are more likely to be full of quiet misery, isolation, and despair.

Once in a while, an Al-Anon's story can be humorous too, but in my experience, it rarely is. I think that's because we try to tell our stories, not the stories of the loved ones who brought us in. In fact, as newcomers, we are gently told to focus on ourselves, not the alcoholic. That's what I try to do in this chapter, and the result is, unfortunately, a pretty bleak tale. But, be patient; it gets better.

I need to start with some ugly facts

My family history in America goes back five or so generations. There is evidence that, despite their successes, broken people, alcoholics, and codependents who loved them were liberally sprinkled among the hundred or so men and women who are my historical family in America. Further back, whatever defects they had and the consequences they suffered are lost in history. I know, though, that the spiritual, emotional, and physical damage of addiction, compulsion, and other forms of craziness spread from one generation to the next. I inherited my share, and I know

now that there should neither be blame nor shame attached to that unpleasant fact. My father, a functioning alcoholic, abandoned his family. My mother, a strong, brilliant, loyal, and courageous woman, was an inheritor of the condition we call codependence and passed on consequences to me. She did her utmost duty as wife and mother with love and the best of intentions. Still, I was damaged.

One of the saddest parts of my story is that the damage didn't stop with me. The defects at the heart of my chaos and pain warped and eroded my relationships with my children and, no doubt, damaged them too.

My codependency colored all aspects of my life, but most prominently, it warped my desires and best intentions. Without planning to, I screwed up every serious relationship from teen to retirement.

I chose the women in my life poorly, and they chose me despite, and sometimes because of, my defects. I married two deeply damaged women who drank alcoholically, and they are the "qualifiers" in my story.[2]

It is not my place to tell the stories of the alcoholics. Consequently, in the personal parts of this book, to the extent possible, I focus only on my experience. Sometimes for narrative purposes, I have conflated my experience in one of these failed marriages with my experience in the other. Telling my story in this way may create a little confusion, but believe me, it couldn't possibly be as confusing to read as it was to live!

What it was like

From a distance the external aspects of my life, for the most part, looked pretty good. Broken home, but not impoverished. Good public schools. Useful education. Lucky early exposure to computers and communications technology. Good techie jobs leading to better jobs with promotions and significant advancement. Almost always enough money.

---

[2] My Twelve Step experience has been as a member of Al-Anon, whose Third Tradition says, "The only requirement for membership is that there be a problem of alcoholism in a relative or friend." In meetings, members often refer to the alcoholics in their lives as "qualifiers," the people who made the member "qualified" for the program.

One Al-Anon's Story

Never hungry, homeless, or hopeless.

But up close (even from outside), cracks could be seen. Social life gradually diminished to almost nothing. The family held at arm's length. Career bogging down, hobbies fading, and sports abandoned. The reality, of course, was discernible from the inside, but denial kept me from seeing it.

When I started this book, I wanted to write the next couple of pages in the third person because talking about what "I" did, what "I" felt, and what happened to "me" is (after all these years) still too tender to expose too abruptly. But it all happened, and it happened to me. So, much as I'd like to, I can't step aside emotionally and write about what happened to "him." It's my story.

Glimpses into the chaos

- The deal could mean a small fortune, but it might require moving out of the city. "I'll never move!" She cried, screamed, sulked, and drank. I wanted to please her, so I put aside the rational judgment and killed the deal. Soon she wanted to move out of the city. "I can't live like this," she cried, screamed, sulked, and drank. I wanted to please her, so we bought a suburban house, remodeled it, and moved. She hated it immediately. She wanted to move back to the City. "I can't live like this," she cried, screamed, sulked, and drank. I wanted to please her. We moved back to the city and spent heavily remodeling a new apartment. She didn't like the building, the people, the neighborhood. "I can't live like this," she cried, screamed, sulked, and drank. I wanted to please her, so we bought another apartment in a different neighborhood. At first, no more screaming, just sulking and drinking. I considered this a success.
- She couldn't work, couldn't drive. The baby's cries in the night woke me, but she was too deep in drink to hear. The checks she wrote to the liqueur delivery service became an illegible scribble. I knew all this but still believed her when she said she'd be healthy

tomorrow. It never occurred to me that I was seeing a disease. I thought that all I needed to do was find a way to please her.

- As usual, it was late afternoon when she called my office. I listened to the familiar slurred voice progress quickly from minor complaint to rant as it predictably did. Then, the call ended in recrimination and exasperation. I packed my briefcase, told my secretary I would be at home if anyone needed me. I left the office early knowing two things: these early departures were damaging to my reputation in the firm and that when I arrived home, I would find the little white dog cringing in the corner in response to the inexplicable behavior of her mistress. I knew what I would find but felt compelled to put my career at risk for nothing better than another repeat of my wife's drama of drunkenness and rage.

- I knew it was worse than useless, it was foolish, but I did it anyway; emptied the vodka bottle I'd found barely hidden in the back of her closet. She emerged from her sodden sleep to watch me pour the last few gurgles into the sink. The screaming started, hers and mine. I snatched her keys. She grabbed mine, ran out, and hurried into my car. I stood in back, blocking the drive; "Please don't. Please!" Our eyes met in the rear-view mirror, and she shifted into reverse and drove into me, knocked me aside, and drove off. I was only knocked about and bruised but so angry with her that it was years before I saw my dangerous stupidity, standing between an addict and her drug of choice.

Are you beginning to see a pattern here? I'd do anything to make her happy because her unhappiness led to the drunken behavior. So I would make her happy, and she would stop drinking. It never occurred to me that drinking was the problem.

And then it got worse

- I did what I could: reasoning, humoring, managing the drinking, forbidding the drinking, joking about

One Al-Anon's Story

the drinking... everything I could think of—the usual useless results.

- Then, she said, "I need help. I can't stop." I did everything to get her into the best treatment facility; made the reservations, made the excuses for her, did the paperwork, did the family interview, drove her to the airport, and with a mixture of relief and hope, kissed her and watched her board the plane.

- When the counselor for the family week group at the expensive rehab asked what I would do if she relapsed, I was annoyed and insulted. I insisted that wasn't going to happen. After all, they'd fixed her, hadn't they? A week later, she got lost in a bar between planes on the way home, and the hope I'd counted on vanished, banishing serenity, and crushing my spirit, a sensation growing more and more familiar.

- I closed and locked the bedroom door just to find some peace, a little respite from the rage, a little bit of quiet from the drunken snarls and screams. She pounded and raged. I pleaded for peace; she pounded and raged some more. I covered my ears and sobbed. She screamed about my cruelty, my failure, my unfairness. Eventually, it was quiet. I opened the door and went out by the pool for fresh air and a calm moment. Suddenly she charged out after me. I begged her to leave me alone, but she raged on. Desperation seized me. I lifted her off the ground, surprising her, took three steps to the edge, and gently dropped her in the shallow end of the swimming pool. Sputtering, dripping, and outraged, she called the police. They threatened me with arrest and jail. I never thought someone who loved me could ever abuse me. I never thought I could behave so excessively toward someone I loved.

- One night late, I was feigning sleep and heard her on the phone saying to someone that I had been beating her, and she needed protection. The following day I confronted her about the lies. She denied it, then said she didn't remember, then said she was sorry. She was going to stop drinking that day and go to an A.A. meeting. I believed her and was happy all day until I came home and found her passed out with her uneaten breakfast still on the table where it had been when I left.

- My son was coming for a Christmas visit, and I went to the airport to pick him up. Of course, she'd been drinking, nothing new there. But when my son and I returned, she was sprawled on the floor naked and bleeding from both wrists. Not serious wounds, it turned out, but there was a trip to the emergency room, a 72-hour hold, then another extended stay in a locked ward. My son and I spent a holiday pretending everything was normal..

In the rooms of Al-Anon, they call this pit of despair a "low bottom."

It was getting serious, seriously serious, and I was wounded, frightened, and desperate..

- When I went to a shrink because I was afraid I was coming apart, she eventually suggested Al-Anon. I objected. Friendly people, but they're all a little sick. I said, "I don't have a problem; she does." I resisted the idea of a Twelve Step program, "No, I saw Al-Anon at the rehab family week; it's not for me."

- A typical morning, she was hungover, guilty, ashamed (probably sick and frightened); I shouted at her, "Can't you see, you're throwing my life away one day at a time!" It simply didn't occur to me that I was the one throwing away my own life one day at a time.

- The turmoil on the inside began to slop over more and more into the good-looking outer life. Gradually I lost my confident demeanor. Then I lost my concentration. Then I lost my job, my home, my savings, my self-respect. I was living separated from her in a cookie-cutter residence hotel. I came back to that sterile room one evening, sat in the chair by the window, head in hands, and cried. Little sobs, then bigger sobs, then moans and cries, and finally quiet again.

I was so lonely, so hollowed-out, so isolated and vulnerable, and the emptiness was physical pain. One place I knew would take me in, one place that might welcome or at least tolerate me. So I dried my tears and headed out. It was June 1999. They say that a journey of thousand miles begins with a single step. This was my single step. There would be twelve more.

What happened

I guess you know what happened to that battered and damaged fellow. I went to an Al-Anon meeting.

I don't remember anything of the content of the meeting, but I remember fondly the two members who sat outside with me on the building's steps afterward as I blundered and blubbered through my story and pain. How patient they were! I later discovered that my listeners were a long-term Al-Anon and a long-term A.A., Twelve Step veterans holding up my spirit when it felt trampled by the world.

Later, driving back to the hotel, I felt better than I had before the meeting. So, being a (sometimes) sensible person, I went to another meeting the next day. Again I felt better on the way back. That's how it started.

Starting the climb up to the Steps

When I first came to Al-Anon, dealing with the alcoholic absorbed all my energy. My career was failing, but it was easy to blame that on business partners. I was estranged from my family but hardly felt the emptiness because I was overflowing with anger and fear. I shouted. I schemed, I sulked. Sometimes I sobbed.

I felt entirely isolated and had no energy to reach out to anyone except the sick person who seemed to be in the middle of my troubles. In the beginning, I had no understanding of the roots of my pain. I had no idea how deep my wounds were. I was utterly unable to see that something was wrong with me.

I don't know how many meetings I went to before it occurred to me that the wall poster with the Twelve Steps might be addressed to me. Even though it says right in the Al-Anon suggested welcome that the program is "based on the Twelve Steps (adapted from Alcoholics Anonymous), which we try, little by little, one day at a time, to apply to our lives ..."[3] It took a while before I could hear it. Still, eventually, I began to pay attention to the Steps and to consider applying them to my situation. But, *No*, I thought to myself, *No way!*

I was going to meetings because there were people there. It was a break in my isolation. The people were friendly. There were hugs.

On the other hand, there were the Steps ... and they were beginning to seem an unavoidable hurdle. This program (which I was so well-qualified for) was based on reading and doing the Twelve Steps. My cursory reading of the Steps had left me cold. I could see the possible line of thinking that had led to writing these things down. I looked up the story about Bill W. and the early history of A.A. But why should I do these things? Why were so many people talking about these oddly worded Steps with such reverence and interest? Why put so much focus on the exploration and explanation of 212 words quoted from an old book.

Miserable as I was, I became intrigued and began to think about the Steps ... and me..

One thought, one small act, one "aha" moment led from one to another. I went to meetings. I listened. I read the literature. I thought some more. More or less, without knowing it, I started to do the Steps. In a month or so, I decided to get a sponsor.

I will describe some of my personal experiences as we go along, but this book is less about me and more about the Twelve Steps and where they've taken me. For now, let's just say I did the Steps. After a while I did them again. Then I discovered that there were parts that I had to do often, some every day. Over the years I helped others who were doing the Steps or wanted to do the Steps or who were troubled about the Steps.

---

3 *How Al-Anon Works* p.9

After several years, I came back and did the Steps consciously and in order again. I talked about the Steps in meetings. Read about the Steps in a lot of recovery literature. I wrote what was intended as a scholarly article about the Twelve Step program.[4]. I had conversations about the Steps with people who were curious about my experience. Some understood; others didn't—a few were openly skeptical or dismissive. I even had chances to speak at length about the Steps to Twelve Step audiences.

While all of this was happening, life went on. Things got worse, then better, then worse, then better, the way life does. All the while, the "worse" got a little better, and the "better" got better too. The promises came true.

What it's like now

Peaceful, that's what life is like now. Oh, there are the occasional flare-ups, blow-ups, and screw-ups, but the background — the framework of my life — is peaceful, quiet, calm. What an enormous contrast to the chaos, clamber, and confusion that once were the background music and foreground facts of my life.

I live now with a wonderful woman who is also in recovery. In our marriage, we have a great serenity. Each morning with our coffee, we read recovery literature to each other. The readings often provoke a discussion, or a memory, or a laugh. Often we tell each other how grateful we are ... for each other, for the good life we have, and for our Twelve Step programs.

Sure, there are still struggles; life keeps happening. Fear, anger, or frustration sometimes take over, and I can feel the old feelings again; that's scary. And there is still heartbreak around frayed relationships with my children and friendships lost from neglect. Today, though, I have a repertoire of insights and tools that I can use to get back my sound judgment, my rational thought, and my healthy perspective. These are the things I "recover" in my recovery.

My life is large now. Not dollars-wealthy or things-rich, but large with an awareness of life's spiritual dimension

---
4 Graduate student paper, *Twelve Steps and the Eight-fold Way*, July 2000.

and the enormous range of possibilities that are mine to choose. I have decided to investigate, study, and attempt to master skills that my old life had no time for. In those days, I was intensely focused on the drama of my loved one's addiction, and there wasn't even time for the necessities of life. Now I find great pleasure in my amateurish attempts in music and art. Now I find time for participation in the simple society of my small neighborhood. Now there is time for peace, for study, for enjoyment, for work, for rest, for love, and for laughter. Now I have a life.

These last few paragraphs would have been a very great surprise to the man who attended that first Al-Anon meeting. If he could have understood them at all, he would have been quietly scornful, only politely agreeable, and implacably skeptical. Underneath thick layers of denial, he would have been painfully envious. From today's perspective, I see that all the sophistication, education, and experience that I brought to that first meeting were helpless in the face of the disease. Several thousand times since then, I have stood in a Twelve Step meeting circle, holding hands and sharing in a prayer that ends with a hearty "Keep coming back. It works if you work it!"

It does.

The Twelve Step Waltz

IN AL-ANON WE OFTEN HEAR ABOUT THE THREE As, a traditional message referring to Awareness, Acceptance, Action. At a very large scale, from 10,000 feet so to speak, I look at a Twelve Step program in those three-A terms:

- The first few Steps are about Awareness and bringing my situation into rational focus.

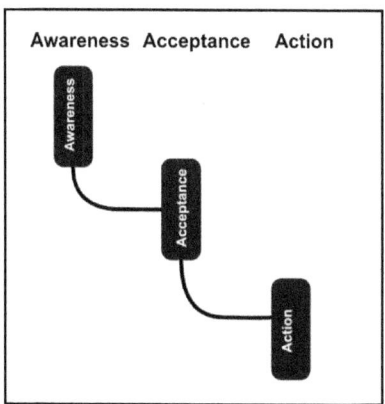

- Then when I take more Steps, my conscious mind begins to provoke emotional changes in my subconscious. I experience Spiritual changes as profound Acceptance of the reality I live in.

- Finally, the last few Steps prescribe Actions that I take to inspire and magnify a spiritual awakening and give me the motivations and habits of a seeker on a spiritual path.

In the following sections and chapters, we will talk about the Steps a few at a time. In a sense, each Step has its own three As. First, thoughtful awareness of ourselves emerges. Second, we marinate our minds in awareness until we can grasp and accept the critical reality of ourselves and our situation, then we can take appropriate Action. Some Steps are more about the Awareness part. Others are more about the Actions. Finally, in all the Steps, we work to get more clarity about what's real. That's Acceptance: a firm grasp of reality.

All the Steps come from the A.A. Big Book.[5] Bill W., the

---

[5] I will refer to *Alcoholics Anonymous, The Story of How Many Thousands of Men and Women Have Recovered from Alcoholism* as the A.A. Big Book.

A.A. Big Book's author had a laser focus on describing how those who suffer from alcoholism can find relief from addiction and recover their lives. For me, the first three Steps were all about seeing reality clearly and coming to understand that it's a lot bigger than I thought.

Step One

We admitted we were powerless over alcohol—that our lives had become unmanageable.

Well, we've got to start somewhere, and this is it: the first part of Step One and its hurdle: powerlessness over alcohol.

I just about quit before I'd even begun because I felt I was better than this. Alcoholics were damaged, pitiful people. Sure, they were powerless. But, it was insulting to expect me to put myself in the same category as the sad, broken woman who had driven me here.

I said, "I don't have a drinking problem; she does. Therefore this powerlessness thing just doesn't apply to me!" That's what I thought. So, right off the bat, I put an overly literal interpretation of Step One squarely between me and the possibility of recovery.

I looked around in my meetings and saw other pretty smart people unconcerned about this little detail. How did they do it? How should someone like me interpret this Step? This was going to require some thinking.

Some people get to the foot of the Twelve Steps because of alcohol. One day a drunk says to someone (even if no one's around), "I can't stop. I need help." That's a pretty straightforward way to read the first part of Step One, and it is probably precisely what Bill W. was talking about when he wrote it.[6]

If I am an alcoholic, the phrase is specific and literal. If I have an addiction to some other substance like heroin, the parallel between intoxicating substances is pretty straightforward, and the inference is obvious. Likewise, if

---

[6] Bill W. was the leading founder of Alcoholics Anonymous and the principal author of the Twelve Steps. The Steps first appear in the A.A. Big Book originally published in 1939. Alcoholics Anonymous and A.A. are registered trademarks® of A.A. World Services, Inc.

the compulsion that damaging my life is behavior such as gambling, the substitution of the addictive behavior for "alcohol" is easy enough to understand. One way it gets complicated is when I need to recognize a certain powerlessness over an activity that isn't ordinarily optional, think eating (as in over-eating) or sex (as in sexual addiction). Other Twelve Step programs have chosen to modify the wording in Step One to be specific about the particular daemon they are fighting — sex addiction, narcotics, heroin, overeating, and a long list of other compulsions. But, all in all, powerlessness over a specific substance or behavior is straightforward to understand.

On the other hand, in my case, I got here because of someone else's behavior, not mine (at least that's what I thought then). That belief makes understanding the first part of Step One more complicated. The "powerless over alcohol" part seems strange. She was the drunk, not me. She was the powerless one, not me. I can take a drink or leave it; I have all the power I need over alcohol.

No matter my loved one's addiction or compulsion

— they suffer from it, and I understand why they are suffering, but I don't have their problem. My suffering is different. I can say now, "Yes, the facts were the facts," but at the time, emotional distancing was a part of my denial.

One way to deal with such emotional distancing is to read the phrase this way: "I am powerless over the alcohol he drinks; I can't control the alcohol's effect on him, and I can't seem to control the compulsion he feels to drink it. Heaven knows I've tried." This is most likely the way the founders of Al-Anon interpreted this part of the Step when they decided to adopt the Twelve Steps, more-or-less verbatim, from Alcoholics Anonymous. There is a profound truth underlying the specific words, but getting beyond the literal phrasing is challenging.

This challenge is the first of several similar challenges I encountered. Thinking back on my early confusion, it clearly shouldn't be surprising that a recipe for a better life in 212 words requires a bit of interpretation.

When I first began to think about doing Steps, I went with the version of being powerless over her drinking (I certainly had enough evidence that I couldn't control her). Then I put the first part of Step One behind me and moved on. However, the second part of Step One had additional hurdles for me. It said, "[We admitted] ... that our lives had become unmanageable."

For me, the word "unmanageable" was even more difficult to swallow than "powerless." After all, I'd made a career managing things. I was the youngest ever research director in a world-class consulting company. I was the president of a startup company before I was thirty. I was a VP at one of the world's largest banks. I was a partner of a century-old Wall Street firm. I ran operations and technology for giant corporations. Management was what I did! So how can "unmanageable" apply to me?

After my internal protest settled down, it occurred to me that maybe my confidence in my management ability might be misplaced. After all, things hadn't been working out all that well for me recently. A candid assessment forced me to recognize that my career wasn't working out, my marriage was failing, my relationships with friends and family were essentially dead — not the picture of a well-managed life. Viewed now, from the distance of years of recovery, the word "unmanageable" seems totally appropriate.

Since then, I have not only gotten perspective on my history and the words "powerless" and "unmanageable," but I've also developed an opinion about the word "admitted."

What does "admitted" mean?

My original reading of the First Step gave me the feeling that I was being asked to confess to something. Was there a guilty truth that I must 'fess up to? Must I confess I had somehow gotten my life wrong? And the first Step was about raising my hand and saying, "I cannot tell a lie; I did it with my little hatchet?"

But I wasn't ready to look too carefully at my part in my damaged life. I didn't feel guilty, but the admissions seemed uncomfortably like accusations.

I no longer think that Step One is like that. Now I understand the word "admitted" to mean "allowed in" as in "He was greeted warmly and quickly admitted to their home" or "Admission to the party was by invitation only." Today I believe that what I am "admitting" is a glimpse of reality.

The Serenity Prayer

Over the years, I've begun to associate Step One with a general problem: how should I deal with a situation I don't like? So the familiar Serenity Prayer was the first bit of Twelve Step wisdom that really stuck with me.

> *God, grant me the serenity*
>
> *to accept the things I cannot change,*
>
> *The courage to change the things I can,*
>
> *And the wisdom to know the difference.*

This was the tool that helped me truly get Step One. Here's how it worked.

The Serenity Prayer encouraged me to examine the idea of control.

Imagine I was spending my time, energy, and wealth trying to control the weather by dancing the rain dance, and my compulsive dancing and chanting alienated my friends and family, cost me my job and ruined my health. Wouldn't it make sense to recognize my powerlessness over the weather to begin healing?

Eventually, it dawned on me that much of what I was doing was a lot like dancing for rain. No matter how hard I worked at it, no matter what technique I adopted, no matter my style, attitude, demeanor, or intent — I wasn't going to make it rain. Like the weather, some things, especially my alcoholic loved one's addiction, I simply had no control over.

The Serenity Prayer generalized this powerlessness for me. There were things I couldn't change, those I should accept. There were things I could change, those I should work on. The heart of the prayer (and the practice) was that somehow I figure out the difference.

Summarizing Step One

Step One says, "We admitted we were powerless over alcohol— that our lives had become unmanageable." Here are the big things I came to while thinking about that first Step.

- "Admitting" doesn't mean confessing. It means letting the truth into my mind.
- "Powerless" doesn't mean hopeless. It's a reminder that reality is full of things I can't control.
- When I admit reality into my rational mind and see my life as unmanageable, I open up to the need for help.
- When things are bleak, seeing them clearly doesn't make them worse.
- It's only a short distance from knowing I need help to actively looking for it.

Step One was my opportunity to begin inviting reality in. I admitted the reality of my limitations into my consciousness. I admitted the reality of my current situation. Reality had to break through a layer of denial, into my attention, then into my mind and heart.

At the beginning of my recovery, I started to loosen my grip on a closed mind and give up its self-protection. I needed to hold my ideas about duty, responsibility, and control more loosely. I didn't see this subtle point when I first encountered Step One, but my lack of understanding didn't matter at all. I was still miserable, so understanding wasn't very high on my priority list at the time. What did matter was that even my confused and fuzzy version of Step One opened the door to the next Step.

Step Two

Came to believe that a Power greater than ourselves could restore us to sanity.

It doesn't seem quite fair that the most challenging parts of a Twelve Step program come for many of us right at the beginning. Often we struggle against Step One. It certainly wasn't easy for me to think of myself as powerless or my life unmanageable. It's a shock then, as soon as these ideas begin to sink in, wham, we are confronted with Step Two.

In the A.A. Big Book, the author, Bill W., dramatically describes his personal experience of Step Two, but he doesn't call it that. Instead, the Steps aren't introduced formally until more than 40 pages later, and then he just slides over the inner workings of Step Two.

This vagueness often shows up in the way Step Two is addressed in the program. Sit in a lot of meetings about Step Two, and you'll hear hundreds of different stories about Step Two — stories of how it worked in individual lives. These various stories all point to a conclusion that something somehow could help us extricate ourselves from the mess that we finally faced up to honestly in Step One.

Step Two is difficult for many of us to confront, but the pro-gram literature does help us with several assurances. For instance, in one of Al-Anon's conference approved books (Paths to Recovery pp. 18-21), we are assured that:

- We may be powerless, but we are not hopeless. We are not alone.
- We have choices.
- No religion is promoted or required.
- Around us in every meeting are people who have taken this Step and have better lives.
- That good feeling we get after a meeting that prompts us to come back is neither an illusion nor an accident.

In a way, Steps One and Two are a matched set. Taking Step One would be terribly discouraging without the possibility raised in Step Two. They are also matched in the sense that they both open our minds and hearts just enough to let in what Bill W. called "the sunlight of the spirit." (A.A. Big Book p. 66)

Both Steps One and Two are highly personal. The "admitting" and the "[coming] to believe" are things that happen inside me. The outside situation and the way I experience and express my changes are unique to each of us.

My Step Two journey

The rest of this section is my story as I wrote it when I was doing Step Two the second time around. By the time I wrote it, I was beginning to feel a lot of relief, and my hostility to the "God part" of the program had started to break down. So when my sponsor asked me to write about the experience, I was willing but still just a little embarrassed that a guy like me — intelligent, scientific, independent — would have started trading doubt for faith. Here's what I wrote.

> My first brush with Al-Anon was while I was attending the family program at the Betty Ford Clinic. We were encouraged to attend Al-Anon meetings while we were there, and I went to two quite different meetings, and I was pretty uncomfortable in both. I squirmed at the talk about God and "Higher Power."
>
> I thought that the people talked about "Higher Power" instead of God because it was in some way more politically correct — after all, there were people who had allergies to God, and they have rights too. So I thought that using the phrase "Higher Power" was pretty much just a dodge, and I wasn't having any (thank you very much!).
>
> I thought I knew plenty about God. I'd read the holy books and the theology and the philosophy, and I knew a lot about comparative religion. But, looking back now, I doubt I knew nearly as much as I thought I knew; I've learned it isn't easy to have much fundamental understanding about religion without some spiritual experience.
>
> I always felt that the existence of God was obvious and, the more you look and learn about the universe, the more obvious God becomes. Big bang, cosmic inflation, fundamental forces just the right strength to produce heavy elements and galactic clumps, basic mechanics and relativistic mechanics that make suns, black holes and planets like ours, chemical reactions that self-organize the simplest things into increasing complexity, dynamic processes

The Twelve Step Waltz (Steps 1, 2, 3)

that persist and grow, DNA, chaotic natural selection, self-reference, monkeys, my mother and me — and that's just what we've learned in the last hundred years or so — too fantastic, too wonderful, too subtle to be an accident!

So I believed in a creator or a creative force. I was willing to call it God for convenience, but, given what I believed about God and knew in detail about myself, I assumed that He was too important and too distant to have any personal interest in me. I believed that I was of less importance to God than the details of the magnetic domains turning on and off in a computer's memory or the molecules in the printer's ink on the page are to me. I figured that I'd get rolled back up into God when I died, but until then, I was pretty much on my own. I thought that people who believed in an angry punishing God or a Santa Claus God were silly and philosophically less sophisticated than someone who believed in a coyote god, a rain god, and the Great Spirit Mountain. Sometimes, though, I could imagine how comforting a personal God must be. Too bad I was too smart to have one.

So I believed in a creator or a creative force (I was willing to call it God for convenience) but, given what I believed about God and knew in detail about myself, I assumed that He was too important and too distant to have any personal interest in me. I believed that I was of less importance to God than the details of the magnetic domains turning on and off in a computer's memory or the molecules in the printer's ink on the page are to me. I figured that I'd get rolled back up into God when I died, but until then I was pretty much on my own. I thought that people who believed in an angry punishing God or a Santa Claus God were basically silly and philosophically less sophisticated than someone who believed in a coyote god, a rain god, and the Great Spirit Mountain. Sometimes, though, I could imagine how comforting a personal God must be. Too bad I was too smart to have one.

As you can see, I was deeply troubled. I had been dealing alone with active alcoholism in some form or another all my life. The fight against the disease wasn't working. My marriage, my job, my family, none of these were working. My life wasn't working.

> It was evening in the residence hotel room. I was just back from an Al-Anon meeting. My shoes were off. I had heard in the meeting from a woman who explained that for a while, she had made her God too small to help her with her life. The words hadn't had any particular impact when she spoke them — just another Al-Anon talking the weird way they do.

There is a lot of talk in Al-Anon meetings that uses the vocabulary of metaphor, often religious metaphor, compounded with some jargon peculiar to Twelve Step programs. The words "Higher Power" and "God" are often used interchangeably and totally without any generally agreed meaning. Likewise, words like spiritual, spiritual awakening, defect of character, wrongs, harms, detachment, acceptance, and shortcomings are used without any express agreement about what they mean. This is a strength of the program, not a defect. I make an effort in this book to rationalize the vocabulary according to my own understanding, but a fundamental concept is "take what you like and leave the rest."

So, to continue with my experience that night.

> The woman's words came back to me and played through my head until they got my attention. I wondered, what if that was what I had done. My God wasn't small, but He certainly was far away. What was there about my understanding of God that kept Him at such a distance? Today I'd say that it was only my evaluation of my unworthiness that held Him off; it was only my pride and arrogance that forced me to go it on my own. At the time, I didn't think about that.[7]

> What I thought about, instead, was how comforting it would be to have God up close and personal. I was

---

[7] Twenty years later, I'd just say that I wasn't ready.

hurting. Tears came when I considered what it might be like to stop being alone, to stop being afraid. So many people have that personal kind of a God; what would be so bad about just giving it a try? What did I have to lose ... my isolation? [8]

What is it, I asked myself, that gives people this sense of closeness to God? I had no experience from which to judge what happened inside people who had that kind of faith, but I did have a pretty good idea of what they did as viewed from the outside.

They prayed.

Much to my surprise and totally out of left field, prayer turned out to be the difference.

I never prayed, except the expletive-deleted kind and the kind you say when you might have been killed and weren't — the kind of prayers that happen without thinking. No, I didn't pray, but people who had the kind of God I wanted did pray. In every culture I knew about, there was prayer and meditation and ritual. I knew and had experienced the value of ritual, but I was convinced (still am) that ritual serves to bring people together rather than to bring people to God. I put ritual on the shelf and thought about prayer and meditation.

I knew a bit about mediation. I had practiced meditation as a stress reliever for years. I knew the quieting effect it had on me — how it slowed my breathing, slowed my heart, lowered my blood pressure, and slowed the frantic chasing in my mind. I was a fan of meditation (still am), but I knew it well enough to know that meditation wouldn't give me what I wanted. That left me thinking about prayer.

God didn't need the prayer, so prayer must serve a purpose for the person doing the praying. Prayer in almost all faiths and traditions was pursued in some particular posture and with signal gestures

---

[8] Today, I would say that the source of my pain was less the isolation than the unbearable weight of responsibility I felt and the sense of failure I had because I wasn't able to live up to my own expectations.

— kneeling, prostration, rocking, kowtowing, lotus, etc. So many people do that sort of thing when they pray; there must be a reason. The only reason I could come up with is that it works better that way. As a logical step, that was pretty important for me. If kneeling and so forth makes praying work better, then fundamentally, it must be true that it works! It had to work for it to work better, right?

I thought that special postures for prayer probably worked by calling on some primitive aspect of our DNA, someplace in the mammal-brain between what we share with dogs and what we share with apes. I suspect there is a chemical trigger of some kind that subtly changes our perception when we kneel. Our defenses are down, and we are more open. At least that was the hypothesis that crossed my mind as I leaned back in my recliner chair and thought about how to get something that I desperately wanted. The thinking was going on at one level, and the desperation was at another. It was the pain that got me out of the chair and onto my knees ... and I started talking to God. Spiritual awakening, first hint.

Then, I got a special gift from my Higher Power.

I talked in prayer awkwardly that first night, but I kept doing it. Later, after a couple of weeks, I was sitting on the couch reading, and something I read, a phrase, stuck in my mind — "God, today I give my will and my life over to your care. All is well." Something about the wording felt good. I liked the "all is well" part especially. It was in the back of my mind as I read for another hour or so, and when I put down the book, I thought about it and wanted to go back and find the exact quotation and context.

I scanned what I had been reading and didn't find the quote. I checked in the other books I had at my side that day, but I couldn't find the passage in any of them. Intrigued, I carefully scanned each page of each of the books in the pile by my side, but I never found where the phrase had come from (still haven't).

Somehow God put a prayer in my mind and hid from me the process used for getting it there — a very clever way to underline something. One of a lot of little miracles that started happening to me.

That phrase became a mantra for me. I repeated it, chanted it, and focused on it as the words rolled off my tongue. I focused on the phrases one at a time by emphasizing them differently as I chanted. After a while, I began to merge my meditation with my prayers. This stuff was beginning to get way cool!

Something wonderful, indescribable, inexplicable happened.

Not too many days after I started using this prayer in my morning meditation and prayers, I was in bed alone at night and had just put down my book but had not yet turned out the light. Somewhat fancifully, I thought about saying goodnight to God. I remember saying aloud, with no conscious thought about it, "This morning, I asked you to take care of me ..., and you did. Thank you." The words came out of my mouth, but I heard them as if they had been spoken by someone else, and, as the words registered with me, I knew absolutely, without any doubt, that they were true and vitally important.

The realization that someone had taken care of me was so profoundly touching, so incredibly welcome, and so unexpected, I burst into tears of joy and relief.

I sobbed and sobbed as an unfamiliar feeling of enormous freedom and safety flooded through me. I wasn't alone. I didn't have to carry the world anymore, not even one more step. Something cared enough about me to take care of me. It wasn't a promise or a theory. It had just been proven — something had taken care of me that day, and I knew it without any hesitation or doubt. And I knew it would happen the next day too; I only had to ask. Even years later, it chokes me up to write these words. There is no adequate way to express how grateful I am. Spiritual awakening, a big hint.

> *This is a long way around to explaining that I came to believe that a power greater than myself not only could but actually would take care of me. The shocking thing to me is how fast this had happened. I guess it was a matter of nearly sixty years of pent-up demand.*

That's what I wrote fifteen years ago. I came to believe through a very personal path. It was a journey taking place mainly in my head. I suspect that that is the usual way. Your details will be different, but this first part of Step Two leaves us all in pretty much the same place — with a Higher Power. The rest of Step Two is about our aspirations to have a better life.

Getting comfortable with insanity

It seems to me that if I can believe that some Higher Power, call it God, is taking care of me, it's no big deal to think that He can restore me to sanity.[9] Of course, there is the minor difficulty that I have to admit that I'm presently insane to be restored to sanity. Not an easy hurdle.

I'm sure that the original use of "sanity" in A.A. meant a combination of mental, physical, and spiritual health, and I now read the word "sanity" in its old meaning of "health" rather than the narrower "mental health" that is our current usage. One place where I have to hedge the Step's phrase a little, though, is with the word "restore."

I had grown up in a damaged household from childhood and, as an adult, had been living in the chaos of intimate relationships with alcoholics for nearly 30 years. So what did "restore" mean?

I'd admitted in Step One that my life had become unmanageable. But what can I say about how screwed-up I was even before I spent years with sufferers of addiction and compulsion? I don't think being restored to the particular kind of nut-case I was at 25 was what I wanted or what the writers of the Step had in mind.

---

[9] I am using "God" to stand for my Higher Power I frankly don't understand. No further implications should be drawn from my use of the word. It's a convenient way to refer to a great mystery.

I believe that this Step targets a complete fundamental kind of mental, physical, and spiritual health, call it "original health," that is possible for human beings that we rarely, if ever, achieve because life and our choices get in the way. I began to believe that a Higher Power could restore me to a state closer to that original health than I had ever been. So one of the critical promises inherent in Step Two is that we can not only get even, we can come out ahead — we can become better than we ever were.

What is this "original health," and how will I recognize it when I see it? Here are a few thoughts.

- Original physical health means that my defective thinking will no longer alter the trajectory my body takes through life from birth to death.
- Original mental health means that I can clearly tell the difference between what is happening now from what I remember or what I expect.
- Original spiritual health is harder to wrap my mind around. If original spiritual health means perfect integration with my Higher Power, then original spiritual health is probably not likely for most of us. Original spiritual health for ordinary people is more likely to be "as good as it gets for a living human being." How good does it get? I don't know.

History and literature describe the strengths and contributions of individuals with an unusual capacity for spiritual health vividly. We call them saints, prophets, and saviors. On our best days, we imagine a world that might be if we each had more of what they had. Consider the Beatles' song Imagine.[10]

Step Two invites me to a new struggle

The hope I found in Step Two dispelled the gloom that Step One brought, but nothing comes for free. Part of the price for believing in a Higher Power is an increased concern about the nature of evil. As long as my God was in a galaxy far, far away, I found it unreasonable that He would

---

10 "Imagine" by John Lennon, copyright Downtown Music Publishing.

intervene in the daily events of my life. If bad things happened to other people or me, it was fate or random chance operating. It wasn't personal.

But things had changed. Now it was personal. I could no longer confront the dilemma of good and evil coolly and intellectually. The theoretical difficulty jumped off the pages of the philosophy textbook and landed right in my lap.

What are the logical consequences if now I have a personal Higher Power and I believe that everyone else does too, acknowledged or not. I don't want the Higher Power of my understanding to punish or be indifferent to our suffering, So how do I understand and explain why bad things happen to people? How can my newly-found, personal God who cares about me explain the evil in the world? What will I believe if that evil should strike me?

I wasn't going to resolve this problem inside my Twelve Step program, and working on it, worrying about it, wasn't part of the deal. But it was ironic that the exact change in my heart that opened me to hope dragged my mind into one of philosophy's great debates. It was beyond irony; it was confusing.

The problem of evil is certainly not a new one, and I am far from the first person to struggle with it. Others have been able to hold on to a relationship with a personal God through even the worst possible sorrows and pains — if they can, I can too. I suggest that evil comes into the world when people turn away from the will of God. Although He knows we will, as free creatures, hurt ourselves and each other, that's not his desire. By my actions, I can adhere more or less to God's will, inflicting more or less pain on myself and other people as I act. As I open myself to God, I am less likely to resist his will, less likely to provide the opening for evil. My spiritual strength makes the universe a better place for me and everyone else in it.[11]

---

[11] I am aware that the thinking displayed in the last paragraph is not very sound from a logical perspective. I am well aware that my "will" and God's "WILL" are not commensurate, and jumbling up the concepts the way I have here is not meaningful. So let's just smile and acknowledge that confusion is the sensation my mind gives me when I need to do something creative.

The Twelve Step Waltz (Steps 1, 2, 3)

On September 11, 2001, nine men hijacked four airliners and carried out suicide attacks in the United States. As a result, over 3,000 innocent people died. I was spiritually and emotionally devastated by this act of true evil; most of us were.

But not all the bad things that happen are the result of evil. On December 26, 2004, for example, an earthquake deep in the Indian Ocean triggered a series of devastating tsunamis along the coasts of 14 countries. Over 230,000 innocent people were killed. Again I was deeply affected; most of us were. But even at this horrific scale, this terrible event was different from 9/11. It was a natural disaster, not an evil act.

To my thinking, there is a certain amount of pain and suffering that comes from the simple interaction of us creatures with the creation we are part of. If lightning strikes me, a zillion natural interactions of energy and physics created an electric charge, and my head was the highest thing around ... period. God didn't do it, and God won't stop it from happening. God will be there when I need strength to recover, and God will be there to offer strength and hope to my family if I don't recover.

The question of evil and the Old Testament story of Job, which provokes our thinking about why an all-powerful God allows good people to suffer, are fascinating areas of philosophical and theological inquiry. Still, it wasn't until I opened myself up to a personal relationship with God that they were important to me in a natural, practical way. Suddenly I had to learn what you might call "proper etiquette" and "guidelines and procedures" for conducting myself in this meaningful new relationship—another big hint about spiritual awakening.

Living with a Higher Power

Here's what I say to newcomers who ask me about the details of a relationship with a Higher Power:
- Keep an open mind.
- Don't latch on too quickly to   opinion on this subject.

- Building a good relationship with God is probably a lot like building a good friendship or other loving relationship — it takes an investment of self, and it takes time.
- Don't be in a hurry; the work of building a relationship with your Higher Power is enormously rewarding in itself, so take whatever time is required for God to lead you to that sane, safe, and healthy place.
- Don't believe everything you think.

There is a lot of good news to be found when we put Step One and Step Two together.

- I don't have to keep trying to control things that are out of my control.
- There is help available to get me out of the unmanageable chaos and restore me to a good place I may not even have known was possible.

Summarizing Step Two

Step Two says, Came to believe that a Power greater than ourselves could restore us to sanity. Here are the important points.

- There is a way to repair my damaged life.
- A power greater than I am can lead me to physical, emotional, and spiritual health.
- Such a power exists.
- I can be better than I have ever been before.

I know it's a weird place to find it, but here are some words from the cult classic Rocky Horror Picture Show that sort of sum it up.

> *In the velvet darkness of the blackest night Burning bright, there's a guiding star. No matter what or who you are. There's a light.*

Once I believe that help is possible, it makes sense to seek it out. There's a light out there; I'm going to find it.

Step Three

Made a decision to turn our will and our lives over to the care of God as we understood Him.

Quick review. My life was a mess. Eventually, I brought my despair and loneliness to a Twelve Step meeting. I reluctantly grasped that I was powerless over some things that I was trying to control, and I couldn't manage my life. Thankfully, events, experience, and inspiration convinced me that there was a power in the universe that could help me and make me better than I had ever been.

So what now? This question seems like it almost ought to have a "Duh!" attached.

- I'm thirsty; here's water. So what should I do, drink it? (Duh!).
- I can't; God can. So what should I do, let Him? (Duh!).

It turns out, however, that the Third Step is not quite so straightforward.

What should I call my Higher Power?

First, there is the matter of how a "power greater than ourselves" in Step Two turns into "God as we understood Him" in Step Three. It's undeniable that these two phrases are intended to refer to the same thing. So, why the difference?

When I first read the Steps, before I ever imagined that they might be for me, I thought that this shift in terminology was evidence of a bait-and-switch. First, get the suckers to buy a "Higher Power" and then slip some religion in the back door. I don't think that anymore. Now I think about Pikes Peak.

In 1806, when Lewis and Clark were on one exploration mission for President Jefferson, Zebulon Pike was on another. Pike and his team were crossing central Colorado, and he wrote in his journal, "Today I have seen a mountain that will never be climbed." Later generations named the mountain after him, Pike's Peak, and built a road to the top.

Bird Feet and the Twelve Steps

I lived nearby that mountain for a few years, and it fascinated me. The peak is a constantly shifting drama as the weather, seasons, and time of day alter the light and shadow. They seem to change the mountain's mood.

On a clear day, approaching it from the East, 100 miles away, the mountain suddenly appears, clearly visible. Up close, on a day when the weather is changing, you can see clouds stirring and roiling around it, then it disappears. The mountain hides until the peak pushes through and materializes, hovering and ponderous where there had been nothing. I watched it morning and evening, and it became a familiar, ever-changing part of my life.

On weekends driving west, high up the shoulder of the mountain, I would come to a place where the peak itself was in the distance off to my left beyond a high meadow. From this unfamiliar perspective, the mountain seemed entirely changed. A zillion tons of granite, rock, and snow were transformed because my view was different.

Okay, back from the mountains to the Steps.

I don't think it matters what name I call the Step Two Higher Power I came to believe in. A label is attached to an idea, some construct of the mind. Using a different label may subtly change my mental construct, but the reality behind my thought is as unchanged by this mind trick as Pikes Peak was unchanged by the light, the weather, or where I stood to look at it.

The history of A.A. informs us that early members argued about how frequently and in what way to refer to God in the exact wording of the Steps. What we have is a compromise between strongly religious people and others who felt the gateway should be widened "so that all who suffer might pass through, regardless of their belief or lack of belief." ("Pass It On" p.199) So, another irony: these Steps, which some believe to have been divinely inspired, were ultimately the product of a committee's querulous (and no doubt garrulous) give-and-take.

Maybe before we continue digging into the details of Step Three, we might take a moment to investigate why Bill W. wrote all the Steps the way they are.

Why the Steps are written in the past tense

Many of us would prefer a recipe — do this, then do this, then this, and so forth — but the Steps are not a procedure, not an algorithm, not a set of instructions. The Steps were Bill W.'s record, based on his experience and observations, of what had worked for those who suffer from alcoholism, i.e., what they had done that allowed them to overcome their addiction and compulsions. Hence, the past tense.

Nothing imperative, nothing directive, just a hopeful consolidation of the early members' personal experience. This rhetorical choice embodies a critical foundation stone of all Twelve Step programs. The Steps must be read as suggestions based on the experience of others.

When I undertake to build a better life based on the Twelve Steps, I must recognize that my application of the Steps is uniquely mine, and, consequently, I have both freedom and responsibility. Freedom because I can work the Steps in my fashion in my time. Responsibility because I have to own my choices. Freedom to choose.

And it turns out making a personal choice is the heart of Step Three.

The Step Three decision is a choice

The Step says, "Made a decision ..." A decision is a choice among alternatives. I can do this or that, door one or door two, run or walk, etc. In this case, the choice seems to be "...to turn our will and our lives over to the care of God as we understood Him" or not. Simple as it appears, there is complexity here.

- One choice: Take the Step or don't take the Step at all
- Another choice: Make or don't make this specific decision.

I can choose not to take this Step. If I just back away from the program at this point, I can continue to go to meetings, feel the closeness and support of the group, and experience the good feelings on the way home. No more work is required.

On the other hand, if I choose to take the Step, I have something to do — decide to take the specified action. Note carefully: my action is to make a choice, i.e., make a decision. The implementation part comes later.

I aspire to a goal. Getting there is up to me, and at this point, the "how-to" isn't all that clear. At the risk of belaboring this point about decision making, Let's look at a decision and its consequences.

> *I decide to go to a movie and be entertained for a couple of hours. I check the time and place of the film. Drive there. Buy a ticket. Resist the temptation of movie popcorn. Find a seat and settle in to be entertained..*

In this example, I am pretty clear on the expected outcome, and I know with some precision what I have to do to carry out the decision. So let's try another one..

> *I decide to become an airline pilot to make a lot of money and travel to exotic places. But, unfortunately, I don't know how to fly a plane, and I don't know much about the airline industry.*

In this case, I have a fuzzy (perhaps wrong) understanding of the outcome of my decision because I don't know what it's like to work as an airline pilot and I don't know how to become one. I start from ignorance.

Then, having made this decision, I might implement it by learning about the industry, the requirements for pilots, the life pilots lead, and their skills and responsibilities.

Still, I don't know how to fly a plane, so I have to investigate further to determine what implementing this decision requires: ground school, flight instruction, check rides, solos, and all the other details. I still don't know how to fly, but I'm better informed, and my decision will be smarter.

It's this second example which we should hold in mind when we examine Step Three.

What do I have to know before I take Step Three?

As I mentioned a few paragraphs back, I can decide whether or not to take Step Three. The Twelve Step aphorism for this situation is "I can't; He can. So, I think I'll let Him." And, the bumper sticker is "Let go and let God."

How well do I need to understand the outcome before I choose this Step? How much do I need to know about the consequences? What's involved in turning my will and my life over to the care of the God of my understanding? I didn't have a clue.

I suspect that, like me, most who choose to do Step Three have only the vaguest notion of what life might be like in a Higher Power's care. Probably, like me, they didn't think about it much, just jumped. If I had thought about it, I would have been forced to acknowledge that I had no idea how to do the turn-over-my-will-and-life thing and only the fuzziest notion of what would happen if I did.

I don't usually make decisions to do things I don't understand. I typically try to peek inside any process before I commit to it. If I'd thought about it, I might have asked: What exactly do I have to do? How does it work? How long does it take? What does it feel like?

I didn't ask any of these questions. My Second Step experience with my Higher Power's care took away my usual skepticism and caution. I made the Third Step decision with an open heart and an empty mind.

If I had been asked to articulate my thoughts then, I might have said something about how bad things were and how I was ready to try almost anything to feel better. I might have said that I decided to take Step Three because I didn't see any better choice. The truth is, I didn't think about it, and no one asked.

I didn't have a sponsor or any intimate friends in the program. I didn't seem to need any. From today's perspective, I can see that my Higher Power's special gift — the mysteriously appearing prayer and the way I used it so intensely — was a unique tool that my subconscious used to make this decision before my conscious mind gave it much thought.

So I took Step Three, decided to turn my will and my life over to the care of God as I understood Him. Okay, I said to myself, how do I do that?

We'll get to my experience in a minute. But, first, this seems like an excellent place to begin the subject of Sponsorship.

A word about sponsors

In recent years TV and films have given us a Hollywood version of what an A.A. sponsor is and how the relationship works.[12] But with few exceptions, sponsorship in Al-Anon is still not part of the cultural understanding. (Did you ever see an Al-Anon sponsor in a TV drama?) The A.A. and Al-Anon sponsor roles have the same motivation and value, but there are some significant style differences. So when sponsorship comes up in this book, it's Al-Anon sponsorship I will focus on.

There is no requirement that anyone in a Twelve Step program have a sponsor. If I'm content coming to meetings without working Steps, no one will object. Part of the power of Twelve Step programs is that there is no coercion; do it the way it works for you. However, most people in the program suggest "get a sponsor to help do the Steps." I've heard, "Go to meetings to feel better; do the Steps to get better." More later about sponsors, but for the rest of the book, I will assume that there is a sponsor to share with, learn from, and (as it says in the Al-Anon suggested close) "reason things out with."

Take Step Three; then what happens?

So, back to Step Three. One Al-Anon friend who describes himself as highly verbal and oriented to the written word wrote a personal essay as part of his Third Step work. He's given me permission to use parts of that essay in this book.[13] Here's how the essay starts.

---

12 Dozens of A.A. sponsors have shown up in TV series from NYPD Blue in 1994 to the Sherlock Holmes update Elementary more recently.
13 Of course, I have edited out identifying personal information for the sake of anonymity.

The Twelve Step Waltz (Steps 1, 2, 3)

I thought this Step was easy. I got the "power-less thing" real fast, and (much to my surprise) I got the "God thing" pretty fast too. I'd been praying for help since my first few weeks in Al-Anon, so making a decision to do what I had been asking God to help me with seemed pretty straightforward. Then I started thinking about the difference between a "decision" and a "desire."

The fact is, it was very easy for me to want to turn my stuff over to God. I'd flat had enough of it, and God was welcome to it! Indeed, I very much desired to turn over my will and my life. I'd been beaten down by my overwhelming sense of responsibility for my alcoholics, for my children, for my other family members, for my coworkers and colleagues, for any random group I found myself part of. I was tired. I didn't want to be responsible anymore. "Please, God, take all the responsibility ... and please give everybody clear notice that it's you, not me, that's now in charge; I don't want to be blamed if you screw it up." Yup, I had a clear desire to turn stuff over.

Like Augustine prayed to be a saint, but not yet; I was ready to turn my will and my life over to God, but not quite all of it. The confusion started in the details.

When I first saw this essay, I was amazed. This was precisely what I felt. My friend was confused about the details. So was I. They say that God (and the devil) are in the details, so we have to look at those details. In this case, we examine what I should expect from the consequences of this decision and, having made the decision, what exactly do I do when I get up in the morning. That's what my friend was facing.

Let's say that I've decided to turn my will and my life over to God: now how do I do it? It's just the decision the Step asks for, but what's the point of making a decision to do something if you don't do it. What if you don't even know how to do it? I can't *make great music by simply deciding to become a great musician. There were details, procedures, and guidelines about implementing this decision that were still a mystery to me. I believed that God had a part, and I had a part, but I was pretty fuzzy about how to decide who was supposed to do what.*

I think this kind of confusion is common when we come to Step Three. It's easy to get tangled up in deep conjecture about God's Plan, what it is, how I can discover it, and so forth. Here in Step Three, however, it seems to me that all I need to understand is that, if I allow it, my Higher Power will care for me and the way I demonstrate my cooperation is to do the rest of the Steps. By the way, my friend and I came to exactly the same conclusion: **God's part, care for me; my part, do the Steps.**

Summarizing Step Three

Step Three says, Made a decision to turn our will and our lives over to the care of God as we understood Him. Here's what I try to remember.

- This Step is a leap of faith — no net, no guard rail.
- I probably don't know how to turn over my will and my life.
- Even so, I decide to do it (or try to do it or work at doing it or just hope I can do it).
- No particular religion or creed is required.

The fundamental commitment I make is to continue with the Steps.

How this feels

One, two, three. One, two, three. That's waltz time, and the rhythm repeats until the music ends.

When I first read the Steps, my impression was (naturally, I think) that following the program meant doing the Steps (in order), working on each one until moving on to the next. I suppose, in the historical context of bringing sobriety to suffering alcoholics, this impression was precisely what was intended. In my opinion, though, important as relief from addiction is, there are even more potential benefits from the Steps.

In reality, hidden behind the chaos of an addiction, is the truth that my drug of choice is simply a deep desire to control one of an infinite number of things over which I am powerless and which, if I attempt to control them, can bring me injury, misery, and even death. Remember I said earlier, "getting beyond the literal phrasing is challenging." Let's look a little deeper.

Powerlessness is not limited to alcohol

My sponsor told me, "Being powerless is only a problem if you want power." Here's a small example.

I once bought a house whose best feature as far as I was concerned was the remarkable view of mid-town Manhattan from the front windows. I bought the house in the daytime, of course, and I was agitated when we moved in, and I found that every night my next-door neighbor parked his large cargo van directly in front of my new house, completely blocking the view.

I stewed about it. Talked to the neighbor about it. Called the police about it. All to no avail. I imagined slashing the tires, hiring a towing service, installing concrete bollards. My powerlessness over the neighbor's van was evident, but I was unwilling to admit it. My annoyance turned to anger which turned to rage. I lost sleep. I was in a permanent funk. I never solved the problem, and eventually, I sold the house.

Looking back, I can see that a lot of my distress was simply displaced anger at the many things in my life that were crumbling, but for a time, I was out of my mind about a dirty white truck. How sick is that?

I don't care that I am powerless over tides, continental drift, or the temperature on Mars. I obviously can't control them. But, on the other hand, the behaviors of family, friends, neighbors, or coworkers may be things I care about and over which I believe I have some direct or indirect control. Even a duty to act.

I imagine I can exert my control through authority, advice, instruction, or manipulation. When I act accordingly, human nature, reality's complexity, and the law of unintended consequences often rise up to swamp my good intentions. When things don't work out the way I want, I may double down on my efforts to control others. Not a surprise if their modest resistance swells into rebellion. I may feel frustrated, thwarted, even outraged. I may try even harder, and my good intention spirals into the kind of chaos that makes my life unmanageable.

Here is my version of the deep truth we can find in Step One.

If I am trying to exert my power over something over which I am powerless, I can make my life unmanageable.

This seems pretty straightforward: trying to control the uncontrollable is not sane behavior. The trick is to grasp fully the reality in which I live and not be confused about the extent and limits of my own power. There are things I can control and things I can't. Knowing which is which and proceeding accordingly leads to good health.

Clarity about control matters

Failure to be clear about what I can and cannot control is the cause of boundless suffering. Unfortunately, this straightforward theoretical understanding becomes enormously complex to practice in my real human life. For example, here are a few of the things which complicate getting a clear grasp of the difference.

- *My feelings.* Sometimes I swell with anger or fear, and I feel like I just have to do something. I don't decide or make a conscious choice; it just feels like I must act. The feeling can be powerful. In my experience, when I let my emotions drive, we often go into the ditch.
- *My beliefs and principles.* Sometimes I can clearly explain my actions. Sometimes I can articulate my beliefs and the principles I am committed to. But sometimes, the beliefs or principles are buried in my subconscious, and I may not even be aware of them. The hidden ones can profoundly damage my life.

- *Other people's expectations.* Sometimes I feel pressured to control something simply because other people expect me to. I want to behave correctly. I want to be respected, liked, and loved. Unfortunately their expectations about my ability to control something may be as flawed as mine sometimes are. It may take courage to disagree with them.

It's easy to imagine how I may be driven this way and that to inappropriate, unhealthy, unwise actions because I don't have the clarity of mind or courage to do otherwise.

The Serenity Prayer

The Serenity Prayer summarizes the situation in just 27 words.

God, grant me the serenity

to accept the things I cannot change,

The courage to change the things I can,

And the wisdom to know the difference.

Imagine that "things I can change" equals "control" and the "wisdom to know the difference" means conscious awareness of what I can't control (i.e., over which I am powerless). The wisdom comes when I admit the reality of the situation into my consciousness. So, here we are back at Step One. And that's the way life goes when you work a Twelve Step program.

- Step One. I get clarity about something I can't control by admitting my powerlessness and how my attempts to control have made life unmanageable.
- Step Two. I acknowledge that a Higher Power can restore my sanity (help me make better, healthier, saner choices).
- Step Three. I decide to call on that power by trusting the care I receive and doing the rest of the Steps' spiritual work.

People who have been in the program for a while often talk about new situations that troubled them and how the solution was to go back to Step One. This has certainly been my experience: one, two, three...waltz time.

Onion or butterfly

A little clarity, a little awareness, a little understanding, a little faith, a little detachment, then a little new action — that's the way my progress toward a better life has gone.

They say it's like peeling the layers of an onion — I remove a layer of denial and confusion, and there is a fresh layer underneath. This metaphor has some truth in it. I encounter the same kind of challenges repeatedly but with different subject matter and details. The process of dealing with each new layer of challenge is pretty much the same. The speed and ease of recognizing a familiar pattern and getting to the clarity part are what change. Same onion, peeling faster.

My recovery story started with a lot of heavy lifting concerning my relationship with women. Then, after a couple of years, my focus shifted to my relationships with my business colleagues. In recent years I have made peace with my past in these areas, and today's conflicts and concerns are mainly about the relationships I have with my children. Awareness, Acceptance, Action — layer after layer, I have been peeling my onion.

But I don't like being an onion. I prefer to believe that if I unwrap enough layers, practice the process enough, and get good at it, my Higher Power and I can transform me from a metaphorical vegetable into something I would rather be. I prefer to adopt the butterfly metaphor. When I'm ready (entirely ready), I can transform myself from a metaphorical caterpillar to a metaphorical butterfly. Yes, the changes I pray for are that profound.

I may never get to be a butterfly, but as I cycle through the first three Steps again and again with every new phase of my life, I do get closer to the freedom the butterfly symbolizes. One, two, three. One, two, three — the beat continues as long as life keeps happening. That's the Twelve Step waltz, and I keep dancing.

The Twelve Step Waltz (Steps 1, 2, 3)

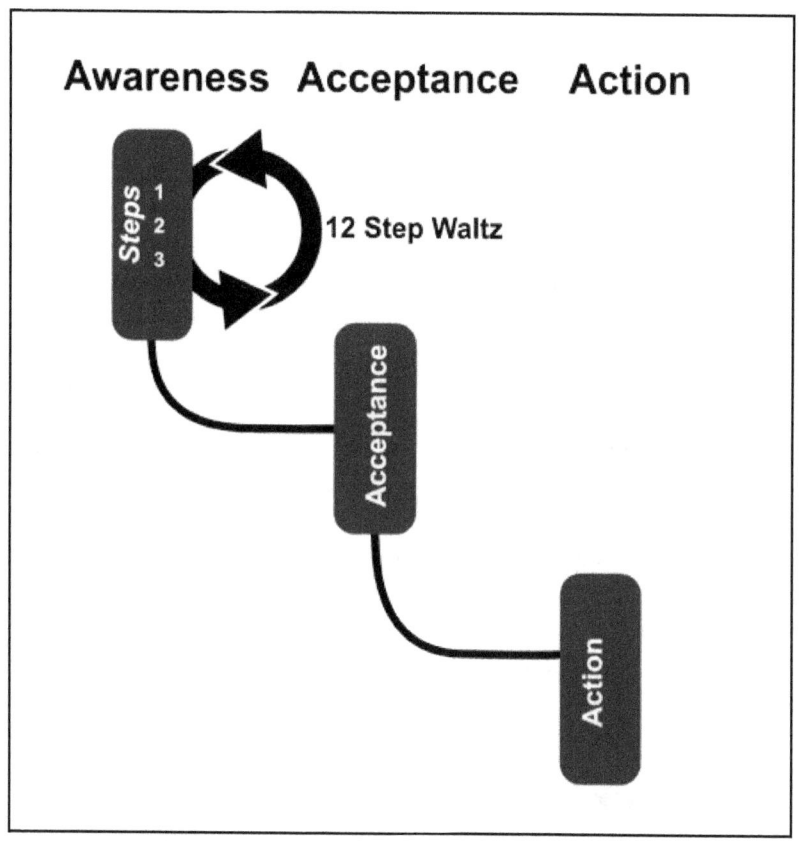

Discovering Myself

IN THE LAST CHAPTER WE TALKED ABOUT the first three Steps, and at the beginning of that chapter, I said that we could imagine the entire Twelve Step program in terms of the Three As: Awareness, Acceptance, and Action.

At one level, the first Three Steps (as a group) are about Awareness, bringing my situation into rational focus. Then, one level down (at the individual Step level), we can see the Three As acting to bring that Awareness about.

- Step One prompted me to be aware of the reality of my situation — what I could control and what I could not.
- Step Two prompted me to accept my limitations and to acknowledge a larger reality.
- Step Three prompted me to act based on an expanded understanding of reality. The Action was to make a decision to continue with the Steps.

These three Steps helped me discover the reality in which I was acting and led me to the next Steps in my journey. The next Steps, the ones in this chapter, begin to provoke emotional and spiritual changes that I experience as profound Acceptance of the reality I live in. These Steps turned out to be about discovering myself.

Step Four

Made a searching and fearless moral inventory of ourselves.

A Step Three decision to go ahead and do the rest of the Steps gets tested right away. Step Four felt like a big deal. I didn't know what I was searching for or where to search, but I felt a strong urge to get on with the work. At the same time, I was hesitant about putting my intimate past on display, even to myself.

The simple fact that the Step says "fearless" suggests that there might be something to be afraid of. And what is a "moral inventory" anyway? In meetings, we hear stories about other members' experiences with Fourth Steps. The stories are often full of laughter about embarrassments and self-revelations. We hear "you're only as sick as your secrets" and give a little internal shiver at the thought that my deepest secret might come out. It's easy to get the idea that doing a Fourth Step just means confessing to every bad thing I've ever done. I can remember thinking, "Confession may be good for the spirit, but I don't do that sort of thing, nope, not me."

Then I decided to get a "real" sponsor. Why the quotes? Well, I had asked a man in the group to sponsor me. He agreed and was kind and generous with his time. He listened to me pour out my troubles. He shared his story with me, and he did his best to help me with Step work, but I never really connected with him. My fault, not his. I didn't understand at the time why I didn't fit with this sponsor, and I wouldn't understand it until several years later and a few serious cycles through the Steps. So I "retired" my first sponsor with gratitude and "hired" another.

More about sponsors

Confusion about Step Four can become a serious obstacle to progress but provides a great motivation to get and use a sponsor. In my opinion, a sponsor has one fundamental job: guide someone who suffers as they work the Steps. That's a big job; we don't have to make it bigger or harder by expecting a sponsor to be a best friend, parole officer, or last resort. My sponsor isn't my boss and certainly isn't my Higher Power.

Now when someone asks me to be his sponsor, I suggest we both pray and meditate about it for a day or two before we commit. Some folks I know agree right away to be a "temporary" sponsor, leaving open the door that there might be a better fit with someone else. I never knew anyone who just said "No."

The general guideline is men sponsor men and women sponsor women because sexual attraction might be a serious complications in the sponsor relationship. In my opinion, we probably ought to stick to this rule.[14] Of course, some of us aren't good at rules, so there are always exceptions.[15] There are probably as many different kinds of sponsor relationships as there are sponsors, and other people need help in different ways, but the best sponsor keeps the focus on the Steps.

The Third Step Prayer

My new sponsor asked me to review before starting a Fourth Step. So, when I shared my experience of Steps One through Three, I got a chance to say out loud what previously had been primarily inner dialog. Also, as we spent time building the trust that makes sponsorship work, I got to hear some of my sponsor's experience as well while I went back over Steps One, Two, and Three.

When I work the Steps with others, We often spend time on the Third Step prayer in the A.A. Big Book (p.63).

God, I offer myself to Thee-
To build with me
and to do with me as Thou wilt.
Relieve me of the bondage of self,
that I may better do Thy will.
Take away my difficulties,
that victory over them may bear witness
to those I would help of Thy Power,
Thy Love, and Thy Way of life.
May I do Thy will always!

These words make a useful point of discussion when we try to share feelings and ideas that arise in the first three Steps. For instance, we can raise and discuss questions:

- Who (what) is the prayer addressed to?
- Do I need to be built or rebuilt?

---

14 Suitable accommodations are made in cases where the people involved are gay or lesbian. For example, I was able, successfully, to sponsor one lesbian woman. In Al-Anon, it is the sponsee who usually selects a sponsor. The responsibility falls to the prospective sponsor to anticipate any such issues.
15 I've had a woman sponsor, and she was the best sponsor I know, and I've sponsored a woman, and we worked together very well. All exceptions, however, don't work out successfully. Sexual tension, exploitation, and role conflicts have no place in the sponsor-sponsee relationship.

- What is the "bondage of self?"
- What difficulties am I asking for help with?
- Do I have any clarity about what "Thy way of life" means?

Of course, these questions are optional, and for some it may not yet be time to look too hard at them. For example, when I worked the first Three Steps with my new sponsor, we didn't use the Third Step Prayer in any formal way, but as I look back, I can see that we did have the level of discussion of these questions that I was ready for at the time.

In the long run, the substance and timing don't matter much but talking about these questions with a sponsor or other trusted friend can banish some of the feeling of isolation that is often part of our suffering. Such comfort is a good state of mind when we turn to a Fourth Step.

The "scary" Fourth Step work

By the time we get to Step Four, everybody has read ahead. Just over the horizon, we see Step Five, in which we "[admit] the exact nature of our wrongs." We begin to worry about what we must include in the "searching and fearless moral inventory." If I write it down now, will I have to confess it later? Maybe I should leave out that part. Perhaps I should just give up on this Twelve Step stuff. Concerns like these challenge my Third Step decision. Trusting a sponsor helps. Taking it slow in Step Four helps. Prayer and meditation help.[16]

Eventually, I get to the Step Four work. What exactly is that work? Well, that depends.

The original Fourth Step

Bill W. described what amounts to a spreadsheet when he wrote about Step Four in the A.A. Big Book (p.63). The spreadsheet has three columns: people I resent, the cause, and the effect on me. He implies another column where I

---

16 Sometimes, we hear that it's okay to take Step Eleven (which encourages prayer and meditation) whenever we need to. Certainly, building my conscious contact with the God of my understanding through prayer and meditation doesn't have to be postponed. (It's okay to read ahead in this book too.)

can list my part or mistake, asking where I was to blame in the resentment. He suggests that we look carefully for the effect that fears play in these situations, perhaps implying another column in the spreadsheet. Finally, he directs our attention to the vital role of our sex lives. He suggests we list all of our sexual relationships and examine them for selfishness, dishonesty, or simple inconsiderateness. He summarizes by saying that if I've been thorough, I will "have swallowed and digested some big chunks of truth about [myself]."

I think that quote is the essence of Step Four. Examine your history. See clearly the events and your feelings about the events, then look fearlessly for the truth about yourself.

Since the first description in 1939 of how to do a Fourth Step, Twelve Step members, sponsors, and authors have tried an innumerable number of different recipes, formats, approaches, and techniques for how to do Step Four. The good news is that the form hardly matters, and they all can work.

Clancy Fourth Step

A nearly legendary A.A. sponsor, Clancy I., has seven questions that can kick-start the Fourth Step for some people. Here's the version that came to me.

- Looking back over your life, what memories are still painful or guilt-ridden?
- In what ways today do you feel inadequate as a person?
- Who do you resent and why? Be as specific and nasty
- as possible.
- What do you conceive to be the ongoing problems in your human relationships?
- What do you consider to be your defects of character as you see them?
- What is your goal in life?
- How can A.A./Al-Anon help you start toward any of your goals?

Some sponsors think a time limit is appropriate (You've got 24 hours to make a list!). Some think questions like these work really well with very tough cases. Others feel that questions like these are particularly useful with newcomers who tend to be reluctant or intellectualizing. Finally, there is an argument to be made that the way an addict approaches a Fourth Step and how codependents approach one need to be different.

Most would agree that Clancy's questions are not quite the same as the Fourth Step instructions in the Big Book. Whether or not answering questions like these is a Fourth Step, or just a way to get started is a lingering argument among A.A. recovery gurus. I'll leave all the arguments to them and just let you decide.

Al-Anon Fourth Steps

Al-Anon, too, has respect for diversity of opinion about how to do a Fourth Step. Still, for those who need or want guidance or structure, Al-Anon Family Groups World Service Office has twice published what amounts to a "how-to" guide for Step Four called Blueprint For Progress, Al-Anon's Fourth Step Inventory. The first version was published in 1976 and was revised and (in my opinion) significantly improved in 2004 (Al-Anon Blueprint for Progress (1976) and Al-Anon Blueprint for Progress Revised (2004)). The more current version is put together as a spiral-bound workbook. After some introductory material, it has 25 sections, each with a series of probing questions. Sections are on topics like Honesty, Responsibilities, Trust, Maturity, and Spirituality. Each section has a short introductory discussion of the quality being examined, often a quotation from an experienced member on the topic, and then questions designed to provoke self-examination.

Scrupulous attention to the questions and complete honesty in answering them will almost certainly reveal a great deal about myself — who I am, what I am, what I've done and why, and what the consequences have been for me and others. Precisely the kind of knowledge that a Fourth Step prompts us to investigate.

My Step Four story and the first Blueprint for Progress

When I was new to the Steps and arrived at Step Four, I was earnest about wanting to do the Step perfectly and not at all sure how even to begin. I had started before I even had my first sponsor. My new sponsor was not exactly directive but made it clear that thoroughness was an important objective.

The first thing I did as a part of my Fourth Step was to write a personal history with an emphasis on relationships. After all, my relationship with the alcoholic I loved seemed to be the source of my suffering. So I wrote, and wrote, and wrote. I wrote my life's history in increments of seven years, emphasizing all the people I had been close to and how those relationships had faired. More than 100 typewritten pages.[17] I was quite pleased with my effort, but somehow I didn't feel done.

By the time I finished that first spasm of writing, my new sponsor had recommended even more work. I bought the first version of Al-Anon's Blueprint for Progress. I worked through all the questions about my attitudes, responsibilities, and feelings of self-worth. Wrote my thoughts about love, maturity, and character—another 50 or so pages. I still didn't feel done, but I had an appointment with my sponsor to go over my Fourth Step and do Step Five. At almost the last minute, I decided to reread the section on Steps Four and Five in the A.A. Big Book. I looked at the Fourth Step approach that Bill W. described and, more out of a desire for completeness than any expectation of additional insight, I decided to fill out the forms the "Big Book way."

Step Four from the Big Book

As I started, I thought of this as more or less a formatting exercise. I'd already done all the introspection, and I had

---

[17] Sponsors usually ask newcomers to Step Four to write in longhand because it is more intimate and possibly more closely connected to our subconscious. Like all of a Twelve Step program, however, there is room for personal choice. Whether it's in pen, pencil, typewriter, or computer file, a Fourth Step is still a Fourth Step.

150 pages to prove it. Doing another rehash of the material didn't seem likely to add much to my understanding. But, wow, was I wrong.

I laid out my feelings, experience, and life's history according to the suggestion in the Big Book. Here are a couple of typical examples.

I'm resentful at:	The Cause	Affects my:
My business partner	He cheated me out of my share	Financial health, self-confidence, trust
My college girlfriend	She lied to me, cheated on me, stole from me	Trust

It didn't take very long. I had just begun filling out the table when the power of the approach began to be clear. In resentment after resentment, the exact words and phrases kept appearing and reappearing in my descriptions of the causes and effects.

There were undeniable patterns in my behavior and my reactions to others' behavior. One after another, these situations had disturbed, damaged, or destroyed parts of my life in similar ways. Until I made this chart, I had never seen my life's dramas so clearly. Each was a thinly veiled repetition of the same sad, misguided story. This was shocking, frightening, humbling.

A Fourth Step doesn't work the same way for everyone. It doesn't even necessarily work the same way for me each time I do it. Each time I seriously address myself to the task of a "searching and fearless moral inventory," I make discoveries about that most fascinating of subjects, me. For me, it wasn't "one and done." Since my first Fourth Step, I have done Step Four several more times.

The new Blueprint for Progress

I had been in the program for more than five years when Al-Anon World Service published the revised Blueprint for Progress. I felt the need to take another long look at myself, so I used the new workbook to guide another broad-ranging inventory. When I compared the new information to the previous Fourth Step, I had a powerful illustration of how my life had changed as I worked the program and followed my path. I had a lot more insight into my behavior, less denial, more honesty. So, in the second inventory, I wrote about how my behavior in some situations had changed.

For instance, in the past, I almost always tried to correct people who made mistakes. Now I had a choice of how to respond. I could respond with polite disagreement. I could say "you may be right" or "perhaps" or " maybe." Or I might even just stay silent. From my first to the second Fourth Step, I became aware that I had this compulsion. Aware that my knee-jerk correction of other people was an annoying habit even when I was right. And, when I was wrong, embarrassing myself, making a bad impression, and possibly even losing a friend. So I was pleased that my action had changed. I had begun to insert a pause between the compulsion to correct someone and the decision actually to do it or not. And, if I did, how I would express myself.

Focused Fourth Steps

On other occasions, I used the idea of fearless and searching inventory to examine specific problem areas in my life. For example, I wrote targeted Fourth Steps focused on my business relationships, my interactions with my children, and even once on my specific attitude about my alcoholic's anonymity. Each time there was new information. Sometimes the information was comforting: I was handling things better. Sometimes there were challenges: I got clarity about how my actions contributed to my difficulties. For me, a focused Fourth Step is a powerful tool.

My homegrown Step Four recipe

In my work with other men, I use an approach to Step Four that seeks to combine flexibility and structure. I suggest that they think of their inventory in five parts:

- Part 1. The A.A. Big Book list of resentments
- Part 2. A close look at fears
- Part 3. Sexual history
- Part 4. Examination of personal assets and strengths
- Part 5. Analysis and investigation of "my part."

Discovering Myself (Steps 4, 5)

I'm not claiming any special wisdom with this approach, but I offer it as one more possible way to work Step Four.[18] The ultimate objective of the Step is self-knowledge, and any tool that works is the right tool.

Summarizing Step Four

Step Four says, Made a searching and fearless moral inventory of ourselves. Here are the things I learned about this Step.

- The Step is not a confession; it's an analysis.
- It's useful to examine and get clarity about my strengths and weaknesses, my achievements, and my failures.
- The format is incidental, but it's useful to use an approach to find patterns in my behavior.
- Once through this Step is probably not enough.

I think I read somewhere, "Action without knowledge is buffoonery; knowledge without action is sophistry." Bill W. may have had some such thought in mind when he ended the "HOW IT WORKS" chapter in the A.A. Big Book after a discussion of Step Four and started a new chapter with Step Five called "INTO ACTION." The Action part is well worth this extra attention. After all, nothing happens unless someone takes action.

Step Five

Admitted to God, to ourselves, and to another human being the exact nature of our wrongs.

Back in Step One, we examined the meaning of the verb "to admit." We get to look again in this Step, and we get to dig into another word that also comes with ambiguity, "wrongs." Other than that, Step Five is simple. Not easy, maybe, but simple.

In our Al-Anon program, Step Five usually involves a private meeting between the member and her sponsor, during which they go over the Step Four inventory. One Al-Anon

---

[18] I've included the worksheets I give out as Appendix A.

sponsor I know just asks the sponsee to read her inventory aloud. The sponsor asks questions, and as they go along, they develop a list of what the sponsee considers "wrongs." This practical approach avoids almost all of the philosophical, metaphysical, spiritual, and religious questions and subtleties that plague some of us. Since I'm a big fan of practical and pragmatic, I'm inclined to endorse this straightforward way of doing Step Five and suggest it to the men I sponsor.

As program members prepare for this Step, I usually recommend that each make their own decision about what it means to "[Admit] to God and to [themselves]" and proceed accordingly. As part of Step Five with the men I sponsor, I ask if they have done these first parts of the Step and if they'd like to tell me about the experience.

It is not necessary to have a sponsor to do this Step. The "other human being" mentioned in the Step can be just about anyone, although Al-Anon suggests that "Experience has shown it is best not to select our spouse, partner, a family member or the alcoholic." (Paths to Recovery p.54)

One long-time member tells of how she was having trouble early in her recovery trusting anyone and when she was ready to take Step Five, she struggled to think of an appropriate "other human being." Finally, when she was visiting a strange city, she picked a clergyman randomly out of the phone book and made an appointment. She awkwardly tried to find the right words to express her request and began trying to describe the Steps when the clergyman suddenly interrupted her, "How long you been sober?" In her relief at being understood, it was easy to share her situation as an Al-Anon and then her Fifth Step. She says God guided her through a rough patch where she had been afraid to go.

Yes, I like the simple, straightforward way to approach this Step, but I also like to dig into some of the questions and subtleties I mentioned. If this stuff appeals to you, too, read on. Otherwise, you may want to skip ahead.

Step Five is not a confessional

My first reading of this Step led me to think about the role that confessing plays in all the world's major religions. There is a robust flavor of "confession" in this Step and reading the word "admitted" to mean "confessed" (in the sense that religions use the term) raises questions like:

- Given confession, what about contrition, repentance, absolution, and penance?
- Is the "other human being mentioned in the Step acting as an intermediary between God and me?
- What exactly am I confessing? Are "wrongs" the same as sins?

It would be way outside the traditions of the Twelve Steps for me to insist on particular answers to these questions. So please take this section as one man's opinion and suggestion.

First, the obvious. A Fifth Step is not a confession in the sense that religions most often use the term. Major religions consider confession necessary for the practitioner to obtain God's forgiveness for his sins. No matter how important it may be to me, the Steps do not suggest that God's forgiveness is obtained by taking Step Five. A few early members of A.A. wrote about this Step and asserted things like, "Acknowledgment of our sins will guarantee us God's forgiveness, thereby enabling us a safe, protected passage down the path of ongoing recovery." [19]They also encouraged confession in the religious sense for members of religions that require it (A.A. Big Book p.74). Nowhere in the Big Book discussion of Step Five is the idea of forgiveness raised. In fact, Step Five is an example of how a Twelve Step program can be spiritual without being religious (also A.A. Big Book p.74).

Given that Step Five is (for some) not necessarily a confession in the religious sense, the idea of absolution and penance don't apply. Repentance and contrition in the popular understanding of regret, sorrow, or remorse are

---

19 Terry D., "The Biblical Roots of Early A.A.'s Twelve Steps,", http://aa-history.com/12stephistory2.html (accessed February 14, 2017).

feelings that may arise as I examine my behavior. Still, they are neither stated nor implied objectives of Step Five. Likewise, the "other human being" need not be a priest or even a spiritual guide. As far as a Twelve Step program is concerned, the "other human being" is not expected to be an intermediary between my Higher Power and myself.

Sin is a word that derives its meaning from religion, as does confession, and what constitutes a sin varies from one religion to another (granted, there is considerable overlap). Wrongs, on the other hand, must mean something subtly different. So when I take Step Five out of the religious sense of confession, I have to examine what the Step means by the "exact nature of our wrongs."

What is a "wrong"?

When I looked back over my life in my Fourth Step, there were interactions with people and things I resented, and there were a lot of experiences that I wished had been different than they had been. I know that I never set out to harm anyone, especially those I love. I certainly never set out to harm myself. But harm was done, and resentments were born. It wasn't that everything was my fault, but when I examined my part in these experiences, I could usually find some action that contributed to the unwanted outcome.

Sometimes my part was central and egregious; sometimes it was peripheral. Looking back on these experiences, it was possible for me to see that my actions or inactions, large or small, contributed in some way to diminishing my life. I could imagine how, if I had acted or chosen differently, the outcome might have been different. I could see how my patterns of behavior contributed to my problems and resentments.

Over the years, I have come to call those patterns unwise behavior. If I had had better judgment at the time of the unwise behavior, I would have made a better, wiser choice. The unwise choices and the consequent unwanted results I now call "wrongs." Now when I read Step Five, I imagine it says "... the exact nature of our unwise choices and actions and the unwanted consequences that resulted."

Admitting things in Step Five

When I "[admit] to God," I am acknowledging the spiritual nature of the Step. No matter how I understand my relationship to my Higher Power, praying about my wrongs places my understanding of them in a spiritual context. I drag the grungy details of my wrongs out into the sunlight of the spirit.

When I "[admit] to [myself] and another human being," I am taking the verb in the sense we discussed in Step One, letting the information into myself. I pay attention to the consequences of my choices and actions and grasp the reality of any harm I have done, intended or accidental. I pay attention to the acts and patterns that have been unwise. I take this Step with another human being for two reasons.

First, speaking to another person, especially talking about specifics I have already externalized by writing them down, amplifies the message to my subconscious. It helps me admit the new knowledge into parts of my mind that are hard to reach and are generally unavailable to my everyday inner monologue. Thinking it, recording it in Step Four, praying about it, and saying it out loud is the Twelve Step recipe for getting it into the parts of my mind where the information can do some good.

Second, the "other human being" part is also there to add context. Usually, the events, actions, and choices that I documented in my Fourth Step feel mine uniquely. Often when doing or hearing a Fifth Step, we discover that our unwise choices and actions are very common. Things that I might have felt too shameful to even think about (much less talk about) are not so strange or unusual as I thought. My wrongs and harms are not so very special, and I am not alone with them.

Whether I interpret Step Five as a confession in the religious sense or interpret it as a spiritual exercise fulfilling part of my Third Step decision, a Fifth Step is a powerful experience for most of us. It certainly was for me. So it's a big deal, and we should acknowledge it.

Summarizing Step Five

Step Five says, Admitted to God, to ourselves, and to another human being the exact nature of our wrongs. Here are the main ideas.

- Step Five is not a confession in the religious sense, but believers are free to combine a Fifth Step with confession if desired.
- We can share a Fifth Step with any other human being, but it's not a good idea to work this Step with an addicted person. Distance is good. A sponsor is especially useful.
- This Step is significant because it gives me a chance to take the Step Four analysis and test it out loud.

I've heard people say that doing Step Five is the real initiation into a Twelve Step program. They say the Fifth Step makes us full members of the fellowship. This is undoubtedly an exaggeration, but it's undeniable that when I have done Steps Four and Five, my commitment to a better life and my decision to turn my will and my life over to my Higher Power are no longer theoretical or prospective. With Steps Four and Five, I have taken some meaningful actions to implement my Step Three decision.

More actions are to come, but Step Five day deserves a big smile and as many hugs as I can gather in celebration.

Commitment

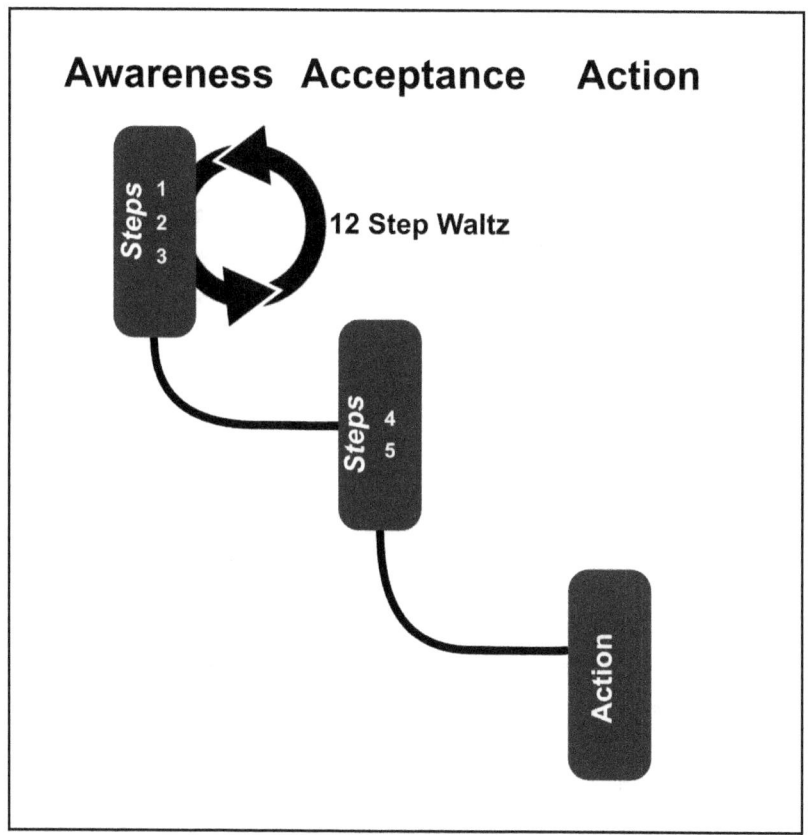

L ET'S CONTINUE TO LOOK AT A TWELVE STEP PROGRAM through the lens of the three A's — Awareness, Acceptance, and Action.

Steps One, Two, and Three are the Awareness Steps. They are the things I did to start understanding the reality of my situation and the existence of a spiritual dimension. Those Steps made me aware, helped me accept reality, and prompted a decision to pursue spiritual help by continuing the Steps. This is personal and spiritual Awareness.

Then came the beginning of Acceptance. Steps Four and Five are powerful tools I used to discover important things about myself. I was internalizing a new reality about myself. This is Acceptance on a human scale.

The following Steps, Six and Seven, are where I make a commitment to change. These are Steps in which I take my Acceptance beyond human senses and into the spiritual dimension.

Step Six

Were entirely ready to have God remove all these defects of character.

The Step itself is not about doing; there is nothing to do. It's about being. That makes it easy to ignore and skip over. And that's precisely what I did.

After I got over the giddiness of working the Fifth Step and settled down a bit, my sponsor asked if I was ready to work Step Six. My response was immediate. "Ready? I'm more than ready; I'm eager. God can have all my defects of character. I don't want them. They don't serve me. Let's go. Onward to Step Seven!"

My sponsor gave me a knowing smile.

I went charging ahead. Step Seven, a little prayer. Step Eight, scrawl a list on the back of a napkin. Step Nine, go and make amends. That's when things started to go wrong.

My attempts at amends failed miserably—hard feelings, new resentments ... a big fail. My entire feeling of spiritual connection began to fade. It was hard to pray, hard to meditate. I had been doing the Steps, going to meetings, reading the literature every day, and doing the service work my sponsor suggested. I felt frustrated and annoyed with the entire Al-Anon program. I had gone off the rails.

It took a while to realize my program was in trouble, and my spiritual path was blocked. As the African wisdom goes, "Do not look where you fell, but where you slipped."

Commitment (Steps 6, 7)

Eventually, I had to backtrack and take a serious look at Step Six.

To understand what happens in Step Six, we need to investigate what we mean by the phrase "defects of character" because that's what Step Six is really about. Obviously, defects of character are things I probably want to get rid of. So let's leave it at that for a moment and first dig into what the Step means by "entirely ready."

I had done the work of Steps Four and Five, discovered things about myself I didn't like and faced up to them. I could no longer deny that I had a part in nearly everything that had gone wrong in my life. There were things I wanted to have God remove, but I had to admit that I wasn't yet "entirely ready," and my program had stalled.

The following section describes what I did that got me going again, but I didn't understand at the time why it worked or really what it meant to be "entirely ready." First, I'll tell my story and then get back to how I understand this now.

Becoming entirely ready

Here are some of the things I learned about myself in my Fourth and Fifth Steps that deeply concerned me. Specifically:

- I made myself comfortable in relationships with others by finding as many ways to be "one-up" as I could. This behavior often annoyed some people and made them hostile to me. Other people were willing to tolerate this behavior for various reasons, but no one liked it.
- These behaviors were reinforced when I sought out positions of authority or attempted to establish positions of relative superiority.
- I did not accept help readily from others, and in turning it aside, I appeared arrogant. That often honked people off.

I spent several days seeking a name for this behavior among the seven deadly sins. Finally, I realized the classic name for this behavior was "pride." The opposite of Pride is "humility," so I concluded that I needed to seek humility to address this defect of character. The search for humility became a key part of my spiritual journey. When I returned to my Step Six and Seven work, I tried to observe this unskillful, unhealthy behavior and substitute humility for my pride, but I was confused about how.

I spent quite a while thinking about humility and pride. I read about these qualities, and I had been meditating on them. I was trying to deal with my prideful behavior, the defect of character I wanted my higher power to remove.

I realized that pride is one of the classic subjects of religion and philosophy (and everyday life). Here are just a few of the folks who struggled enough with pride to write or teach about it: St. Augustine, Confucius, St. Ambrose, Thomas Merton, C.S. Lewis, Mahatma Gandhi, Mother Teresa, Ralph Waldo Emerson, Carl Sagan, Winston Churchill, Abraham Lincoln, and Albert Einstein. I was in good company. I was even privately a little proud of my pride.

After a painful, frustrating period trying to get through Steps Seven, Eight, and Nine, my Higher Power showed me how to work on the pride problem. Here's what happened.

After my Second Step experiences, I had started meditating. Sometime during this Step Six period of frustration, I tried changing my meditation. I would start with simply watching my breath, but after my breathing steadied and my mind began to quiet, I would begin to recite a mantra to myself — breathe in humility, breathe out pride, humility in, pride out … on and on.

One day, after 15 minutes of this, the idea arose that this meditation wasn't working. I was as prideful as ever. I was even proud of learning this specific meditation! My behavior had not noticeably changed.

But as I continued meditating that day, the idea arose that what had changed was my Awareness. I now knew when I was doing or about to do or had just done the unskillful behaviors that continued to frustrate me. I was, at least, aware.

Commitment (Steps 6, 7)

That day or the next (I forget), I was doing a walking meditation. My mind wandered to the pain I felt about this uncorrected prideful behavior. "At least," I thought, "I'm aware of the problems now." On the heels of this modest insight, I realized that I was not only aware of the problem, but I had also accepted its reality and the fact that it arose out of my own deep needs and beliefs, even if I wasn't exactly clear about what they were. I knew that my Higher Power could and would correct this behavior on His schedule, not mine, but I was also aware that I had a part in carrying out His will.

It pleased me to note that I had the Awareness and Acceptance, the first two of the Three A's. That thought drew me immediately to the third A, Action. The idea arose that wimping around this troubling set of behaviors wasn't what was needed. So, I puzzled, "what actions should I take as my part in changing these defects of character?"

Almost immediately, clear answers came into my head. (I don't want to be evaluated for schizophrenia, so I won't say my Higher Power actually spoke to me, but somehow the message was unambiguous nonetheless.) The actions I could take were two-fold:

- Stop talking in meetings.
- Stop offering unsolicited advice.

My immediate reaction to this message was surprise at how specific the directions were and how simple. Also, it felt good, knowing what to do.

Not giving unsolicited advice sounded like an excellent permanent step to me. But, on the other hand, it didn't seem right not to share in meetings ever again.

I was attending five meetings a week at that point. The thought arose that I should stop talking in meetings until December, about six weeks away. If anyone asked me why I wasn't talking, I would explain, but I wouldn't make any announcements. This instruction from my Higher Power seemed very, very clear. The action my Higher Power directed me to do felt challenging, appropriate, and kind. So, I began this modest spiritual retreat—silence in meetings.

I loved sharing in meetings. I thought I was good at it. I thought I knew the Al-Anon line and the jargon. I thought I could be amusing. I thought I could be insightful. I loved having people tell me after meetings that they liked what I shared, or they liked to hear me talk. I liked it when I introduced a phrase or an idea into a meeting, and others picked it up. I liked it when my ideas from one meeting were repeated in another meeting, especially if I got a credit. All this made me think I was a one-up Al-Anon. So, on consideration, it was pretty clear to me why my Higher Power thought I should shut up for a while.

My experiment was pretty much in the tradition of many seekers who struggled with pride — I gave up something important to me and paid attention to the consequences. When my retreat was over, I sat down to write what I had learned from the experience. First, I wrote about the nature of pride.

I learned pride in my accomplishments is not a flaw, and knowledge of my strengths is not a defect of character. On the other hand, "pride of place," as I set myself one-up in my relations with others, is not only a flawed behavior and a defect of character — the whole thing is a delusion! No matter what I did, I couldn't really be one-up. I am what I am, a particular localized part of creation. The ladder I imagined simply didn't exist. Fooling myself about my position with respect to other people made me ineffective in personal relationships and, at best, faintly foolish in other people's eyes.

I also learned about my role and value to the group. For example, many more people noticed my silence than I expected. Some I would never have guessed had not only noticed but commented to me. At first, they thought I was quiet because I was in pain. (More likely, I was in pain because I was silent — this was not always easy for me, especially at the beginning.)

As time passed, a few people indicated that they understood what I was doing, and several expressed to me that they looked forward to the time I would be speaking again. This made me feel so valued and cared for that I tear up a little even as I write about it. Of course, I'm sure that many people never noticed my silence. There may even be one or two who regretted the end of it. The net result for me, however, was to discover that I mattered to that group and I was important to them. I was very grateful for that insight.

I learned my contributions to meetings were real and worthwhile, but they were not essential. Meetings and recovery went on whether I participated or not. When I contributed, it might sometimes help some people, and it sometimes might help me. If I don't contribute, everything I might have said will be said by someone else, if not that day, another day.

I learned about the value of what others contributed and how I sometimes got in my own way. If I didn't waste effort to make a positive impression by sharing, I could hear better what others said. My Higher Power can speak to me through anyone, and sometimes hearing the truth from an unexpected source underlines its importance.

I learned that this retreat had been clear evidence that wisdom is gained through action and interaction with others. At the time, I summed it up this way:

> When we share our experience, strength, and hope, we reflect wisdom and express compassion. Shared wisdom and compassion sow the ground within each of us who listen with the seeds of Awareness. In the light of our Higher Power, the Awareness matures into Acceptance, producing the fruit of Action which leads, in its own time, to new wisdom and compassion. This is how we help one another in Al-Anon.

This was my personal experience, and it's evident that my Step Six story, a silent retreat from talking in meetings and giving advice, is not necessarily what everyone needs. The instructions from my Higher Power were unusually specific and tailored for my personal private way of being screwed up.

Other people are troubled with different issues in different ways. The Sixth Step refers to these issues as defects of character, and the whole point of Step Six is to become entirely ready to have them removed. Simply put, I have to get prepared for my Higher Power to mess with my head.

Diversion about minds

This section investigates how having my head messed with by my Higher Power fits in with the Twelve Steps. The investigation takes us away from the usual Twelve Step topics. Instead of the language of Steps, spiritual path, and spiritual awakening, we will spend a while on the nature of those things without which I am not me, and you are not you — our minds.

Let's agree that we are talking about minds, not brains. Cognitive science, brain chemistry, and neurobiology can tell us a lot about how brains work, and there is no doubt that my mind is implemented mainly by what happens in my brain, but now let's talk instead about what psychology, philosophy, and mysticism deal with, minds.

Let's imagine a straightforward model of the mind that has these parts

- *Beliefs.* A belief is a part of my mind that embodies an opinion or judgment of which I am fully persuaded. Beliefs are intimately connected to the things I think are essential, my values. It's important to admit that beliefs can be true, incomplete, or even false.

- *Mental models.* Mental models are my internal representations and understandings of the things I am aware of and my expectations of how the things inter-act. In aggregate, my complete set of mental models is my world view, my understanding of reality.[20]

- *A rememberer.* The rememberer is the part of my mind that stores and recalls past experiences. We know that this tool is imperfect and selective, but it's absolutely indispensable. The rememberer is the mind-part that is concerned with the first two of the three As. The rememberer is where my Awareness is stored, and Acceptance is integrated with my mental models.

---

[20] Modern philosophy often uses the word meme to label what I call a mental model and the word ontology to represent the aggregate of all my memes to comprise what I have called my worldview.

Commitment (Steps 6, 7)

- *A projector.* My mind's projector imagines what happens "next" or what happens "if." We predict the future, but we know it will probably be different when we get there. Expectations play an essential role in my perception of events and can strongly color my Awareness.
- *A thinker.* The thinker is the part of my mind that uses my mental models, perceptions, beliefs, memories, and projections to make decisions. I experience the thinker as the "I" in my inner monologue and "me" in my reasoning.

My mind combines these parts into a factory to manufacture decisions and choices. The choices drive the third of the three As, Action.

Simpler parts of my brain and body actually carry out whatever actions my choices and decisions direct. Using my body, I walk, talk, work, and play. Actions are the forces that change reality, but the actions start with my choices. Mind over matter is mostly a fantasy, but my mind definitely matters in the case of my body.

Consider one more aspect of this straightforward model of a mind — conscious and subconscious. The conscious mind is the part that I am aware of. It's the place where my attention exists and where my inner monologue takes place. When I am thinking, the conscious part of my mind is where that thinking happens. If my conscious mind is the house where I live, the subconscious mind is the basement. I am not usually conscious of what goes on in the basement, but the basement of my mind is where Awareness and Acceptance live.

The thinker mostly operates in my conscious mind. The rememberer does its work in my subconscious, and when I recall something, the rememberer pipes the memories up into my consciousness. Mental models are stored in the basement and brought to my attention only when I have to adjust, maintain, or construct a thought. Beliefs always live in the basement, and some of them form the very foundation of everything that goes on in my mind. If I want to examine my belief about something, I need to make a conscious effort to dig the belief out of the bottom of my mind before I can see it.

We took that diversion into the structure of mind to get a feel for how the Three As work inside my head. So now we can talk about what I think the term "defect of character" means.

Defects of character

Some Twelve Step literature suggests that the "defects of character" addressed in Step Six are somehow the same as the "wrongs" admitted in Step Five and the "shortcomings" mentioned in Step Seven. It's possible, I guess, that these three phrases were intended to refer to the same thing and the different phrasing was just a peculiarity of the language Bill W. chose; maybe he didn't want to repeat himself. I'm not comfortable, however, with that too-simple reading. It seems reasonable that Bill W., a very bright man, would distinguish these three things only if he meant them to be different.

The Al-Anon literature is imprecise in using these three terms — defects of character, wrongs, and shortcomings — so I'm going to spend some time defining them.

Some Twelve Step members will explain that character defects are qualities like meanness, arrogance, thoughtlessness, or greed.[21] Others will explain that defects of character are emotions like anger, fear, or lust. Neither definition seems quite right to me.

Defects of character are false, misleading, or oversimplified beliefs held deep in the basement of my mind. These defective beliefs are the roots; bad outcomes are the fruits. Voltaire cautions us, "If we believe absurdities, we shall commit atrocities." Voltaire is referring to the extreme kind of character defect. My defective belief needn't be absurd to cause trouble; it's sufficient that a belief be mistaken or misapplied for it to provoke actions that result in harm.

Think about this: we rarely set out to do harm.

---

21 These words aren't defects of character, but they can act as labels for the defects that ultimately cause the behaviors we name with these terms.

I certainly never set out to hurt my Mother's feelings when I ignored her to spend time with my girlfriend. I didn't intend to terrify my six-year-old son when I screamed at him for climbing that colossal rock. I didn't plan to anger my partners when I nagged them about how poorly they were pursuing their part of the business. I didn't mean to set up an angry rivalry between my daughter and my new wife. I didn't mean to enable the alcoholic's drinking. It is rarely my intention to do something wrong, yet I often do. We know what the road to Hell is paved with. So how do my good intentions go so wrong?

I believe that the vast majority of us are always doing the best we can at the time. I think it's better to say that harms usually arise from unwise actions rather than from evil intentions. Using the word "unwise" points me toward the defective motivation for my harmful action rather than assuming a bad intention. I believe that the critical elements of these defective motivations are the "defects of character" I would like to be "entirely ready" to be rid of.

Defective motivation comes from a defective belief

Defective motivations come in a variety of sizes and shapes. Some are simply mistakes. For instance, I may have a faulty perception, or misinterpret what you say, or have misunderstood some stranger as threatening. In these cases, I have misread the writing on the wall.

My sponsor talks about the facts and the story. For example, the fact is that my wife left the house without saying goodbye. Maybe she was simply distracted, or I failed to hear her explanation, but I began to tell myself a story based on that single fact. She's angry with me. She's going to punish me by spending the evening with her worthless friends in that crummy bar. Unless I pretend to be asleep, we'll have a terrible row when she finally returns. I tell myself this story and work myself into a state of jealousy, anger, and fear. Imagine how I feel when, right when I am about to call my Al-Anon friend to rant and rave, she walks back in and says, "I wanted to put gas in the car before we go out to dinner, so you didn't have to worry about it later."

Whee! It's a good thing I didn't take action on the defective motivation that I was building in my mind.

Misperceptions and baseless stories are ways my mind can get off track. Step Six, however, isn't really focused on simple mistakes of perception or the cascade of story I might build on top of simple facts. The deeper problem comes when we hold beliefs about people, things, and reality that are incorrect, mistaken, or inappropriate. Some examples:

- All strangers are dangerous.
- Filtered cigarettes are safe.
- The world is flat.

If I believe all strangers are dangerous, I will severely limit my experience and miss much of the richness of human society. If I believe that filter cigarettes are safe, I may damage my health and shorten my life. If I believe the Earth is flat, it may have no consequence at all unless I need to navigate a long distance. These mistaken beliefs are dangerous but probably not what Step Six means by character defects, even though believing them may be unwise.

What I needed to be concerned with in Step Six were the deeply held beliefs that, again and again, motivated the unwise behavior I saw patterns of in my Fourth Step.

I know that I didn't set out to do harm, produce bad outcomes, or suffer painful consequences, and yet I did it again and again. What motivated these patterns of unwise choices and poor decisions? What untrue things did I believe that took my judgment off the rails? When I could answer that question, I would know what my defects of character are.

Here are some beliefs that aren't true and could drive behavior wildly wrong:

- I need to be perfect to be loved.
- If you really love me, you'll do anything I want.
- I am unimportant, and nothing I do matters.
- They owe me.

Commitment (Steps 6, 7)

One insidious feature of defects of character like these is that I am usually unaware of them. For example,

> Despite the "wicked stepmother" trope in literature, it never occurred to me that my new wife wouldn't mother my children and love them as much as I did. Nor did it occur to me that my children might not be too keen on the idea either. Instead, I had expectations of a rapid, peaceful, and mutually satisfying transition from one family structure to another.

Written out like that, it seems so obviously wrong, but I had only one model of family life in my subconscious belief set, and evidence to the contrary didn't make a dent in my misperceptions or my denial. I wasn't Aware.

My mistaken belief about family, buried deep in my subconscious, blinded me to the trauma and anxiety that my expectations created. Eventually, because of my insensitivity, feelings and events spun out of control. Children, my new wife, and I were in chaos. Mistaken belief led to unwise action. Thus my insanity and unmanageable life.

If I had focused on the subconscious belief, I would have said, "No reasonable person would believe that!" But, unfortunately, most defects of character aren't at all obvious. They are usually hidden and very difficult to correct even when they are identified.

I call these severe defects of character "cracks in the basement of my mind." In my opinion and in my experience, these are the subjects of the Sixth Step.

Where do damaging mistaken beliefs (defects of character) come from?

I suspect that we pick up many of our defects of character when we are children. Our parents tell us things or model behavior that, deep in our minds' basements, we translate into overly simple or mistaken beliefs. It can happen so innocently.

When my daughter was born, I was taken by how beautiful her chubby little baby feet were. During her baby years, I teased her by telling her she had pretty little square feet.

I meant no harm, and my daughter's feet were, of course, perfectly normal, but years later, when she was grown, I overheard her tell her sister she never let her bare feet show because they were square.[22]

It doesn't all come from childhood, though. Wrong beliefs buried deep in the subconscious are not my fault in the sense that I've done something wrong. Sometimes, defects of character can be planted.

Sometimes we accumulate experience as adults that engenders wrong beliefs. For example, a woman in the program told me that she had married a man with a dominating personality. It wasn't long before he started to criticize her actions. He told her she had never learned to do things correctly and never would because she was too stupid. He would say, "It's not your fault you're slow; that's just the way it is. I love my little dummy." A decade of this from someone she loved had destroyed her self-esteem, and she believed she was stupid. She had a graduate degree and had held down two excellent jobs before she was married but now believed she wasn't smart enough to act independently.

When I am seeking to become entirely ready for God to remove my character defects, I need to remember that housing these incorrect beliefs, no matter how unhealthy they may be, is not something I need to blame myself for. Of course, I am responsible for the bad behavior my defects may have motivated, but wrong beliefs are not sins; they are errors.

Getting to ready

How do I become "entirely ready for God to remove" these deeply held, unexamined, and profoundly wrong beliefs? This is tough because Step Six doesn't tell me to do anything. Instead, it asks me to "be" something, and being something or some way is not what my mind's decision factory was designed to do.

Evolution sculpted my mind's memory, projection, and

---

[22] I teased my other daughter by telling her she was "a little old lady in a pink-girl suit." Heaven only knows what consequences lurk in her subconscious!

reason tools to evaluate alternatives and choose actions. But, curiously, it seems that "being" is bigger than my mind can handle. So, if I can't "do" Step Six, what's it all about?

The answer to this question is intensely personal and profoundly spiritual. Two elements combine to get me entirely ready: I need knowledge, and I need faith. I sense some deep resonance here in Step Six with Steps One and Two. When I admitted the truth about my circumstances in Step One, I acquired some vital knowledge. When I "came to believe" in Step Two, I developed some faith. These Steps, even if they were very tentative, prompted me to continue my spiritual path. The same thing is happening, at a deeper, more significant level, in Step Six.

The process of becoming entirely ready involves deepening the understanding of myself I have begun to have due to my Step Four and Five work. Equally important, becoming entirely ready involves deepening my awareness of the spiritual dimension of reality. For example, after working the program for a while, I heard, "The Steps are in order for a reason, but you can always do Step Eleven." It makes sense I'd hear this message in Step Six because prayer and meditation, suggested in Step Eleven, are powerful spiritual tools, and they helped me become "entirely ready."

Summarizing Step Six

The Step says, Were entirely ready to have God remove all these defects of character. So let's wrap up this section with a quick summary of what I've come to believe about Step Six.

My unwise behaviors are not my character defects; thoughtless behaviors are the actions and choices motivated by my mistaken beliefs. Those beliefs are my defects of character.

- The mistaken beliefs (defects of character) often hide in my mind's basement.
- I can begin to understand my defects by looking deeply into my patterns of behavior.

- Eliminating my defects of character doesn't happen in Step Six. It's not something I can do alone but, when I am "entirely ready," I can go on to Step Seven and ask for help.

There are about 100 billion cells in a typical brain. A lot of those cells have to change to eliminate defects of character. So it shouldn't be a surprise that I need help to change them and that, even when I am entirely ready, the change takes time.

Step Seven

Humbly asked Him to remove our shortcomings.

Many things in Twelve Step programs give rise to discussion and differences of opinion. Here in Step Seven, we have another: does "shortcoming" mean the same thing as "defect of character"?

In the last chapter, I spent a lot of time saying that character defects are the deeply held mistaken beliefs that have motivated patterns of unwise behavior in our lives. It seems reasonable that we should be asking for help to get rid of these erroneous beliefs, but no, in Step Seven, we ask Him "to remove our shortcomings." Are "shortcomings" the same things as "defects of character"? Is this just sloppy writing? What's going on?

Let's start by looking at the primary source. We first encounter the problem in the A.A. Big Book where it says, "[Step] 7. Humbly asked Him to remove our shortcomings" (A.A. Big Book p.59). Then in the next chapter, Chapter 4, HOW IT WORKS, where Step Seven is discussed, we read, "When ready, we say something like this, I am now willing ... that you now remove from me every single defect of character ..." (A.A. Big Book p.76). It certainly seems that Bill W. was equating "shortcomings" and "defects of character." For many Twelve Step members, this is enough to end any further discussion. I would never quarrel with these folks, but I have a somewhat different take.

I ask myself, how will I know when a defect of character has been removed? To answer, I think back to how I discovered defects of character in the first place: I saw patterns in my behavior and sought out what incorrect belief might be driving me to do things that routinely spoil my life. Paying attention to my behavior is the only guide I have to deter- mine if a defect remains.

Let's see how this works.

One behavior pattern I identified in my Fourth Step was a compulsion to be correct. I always needed to be the one with the answer. Even if it disagreed with yours (even if you were the expert), my answer had to be right. I could argue endlessly to prove the way I did things was the best possible way. Of course, there were times, such as learning something new or being tested, when I knew I couldn't be always right or be the best at something. I would avoid situations like those with excuses that often ended up making me seem arrogant or reclusive. That behavior turned up again while I was working Step Six. It was a clear pattern, and it was crazy.

At some point in my Sixth Step, it came to me that I had a deeply-held belief that was whispering to me, "If you're not perfect, you're unlovable." When I dragged this belief into the light of day, it was evident that it wasn't true. And it was obvious that this mistaken belief was a defect of character that explained a lot of unwise behavior.

I could see that my natural desire to be loved had been warped into crazy behavior by a too-simple interpretation of a subconscious belief. I can imagine pleased parents smiling and hugging a little boy who could name all the little plastic letters. The parents might have enthused, "That's perfect!" and the little boy might have stored away the experience deep in his belief system ... "perfect makes me loved." Of course, that's just pop psychology, but no matter how the mistaken belief was formed, I was finally aware of it, and I admitted to myself that this mistaken belief was causing me a lot of trouble.

Naturally, I was ready to fix it. But, unfortunately, being aware of the defect of character and the unwise behavior it provoked wasn't enough to make it stop. That's where Step Seven comes in.

Coming up short

As I began to pay attention to my reality, I noticed that one kind of unwise behavior was especially annoying. In some situations, I know what the wise choice is, but I do something else anyway. For example, say I'd love to go ice skating, but since I can't skate, I know I'd look ridiculous at first, so I won't try because I can't be perfect. I know this behavior is unwise and self-defeating, and still, I turn down the skating party invitation. How infuriating!

Why would I behave like that? It seems foolish to intentionally hurt myself by making a known unwise choice. Yet I do it anyway, and I hurt myself. So I come up short of the behavior I wish I had had instead. I think it's helpful to call this particular kind of unwise behavior — I know what to do, but I come up short — a "shortcoming."

If I adopt this meaning of shortcoming for Step Seven work, I focus on reducing the number of occasions in which I know the right thing to do but can't or don't do it. Of course, this assumes some understanding on my part. I must be willing to acknowledge a connection between my behavior and some incorrect or incomplete belief.

In my experience, the defect of character isn't removed like a tattoo; it is healed as I acquire new experiences, insights, and understanding. My defects of character are not just unwanted piles of refuse to be swept away. They are cracks in the basement of my mind. They can be healed, but scars remain.

Yes, I know I don't have to be perfect to be loved, and I'm getting much better at not correcting people, even when I'm sure I'm right; sometimes, though, the correction slips out anyway. So, yes, I know I'll have more fun and a richer life if I'm open to new experiences, but I still sometimes shy away and refuse to give myself a chance to fail and learn.

Recovery is what I call it when I no longer act on one of these incorrect beliefs. I remember the defect of character and what that defect prompts me to do, but I do the right thing instead. As a result, I experience wholesome success instead of doleful shortcomings.

By implication, this reading of Steps Six and Seven puts a lot of responsibility on me. First, I need to see the patterns of unwise behavior, and I need to understand what incorrect belief prompts the behavior. Then I need to continue to pay attention to my choices and decisions as my Higher Power changes me, and my shortcomings are reduced and ultimately removed.

The humility part

Okay, with the definition of "shortcomings" behind us, we now get to tackle the meaning of "humble."

The Step says, "Humbly asked ..." In English, "humbleness" is a modest or low view of one's importance. Humbleness is synonymous with "humility."

It's pretty clear from the wording of the Seventh Step Prayer in the A.A. Big Book that Bill W. used the word humble to suggest a relationship to God while doing this Step (A.A. Big Book p.76). The prayer says

My Creator, I am now willing that You should have all of me, good and bad. I pray that You now remove from me every single defect of character which stands in the way of my usefulness to You and my fellows. Grant me strength, as I go out from here, to do Your bidding. Amen.

I needed to have a proper understanding of my relationship to my Higher Power for Steps Two and Three to make sense; humble is a good word to use to describe that understanding. In Al-Anon, we broaden our thinking about this word to mean "right-sized" in relationship with, not only God but with everyone.

The imaginary ladder on which I place myself above or below you is a spiritually hazardous place. When I see myself as right-sized, I get off the ladder and stand shoulder to shoulder with you and every other person.

Remember what I learned when I stopped sharing at meetings for a month? I called my defect of character "pride" and described my unwise behavior in terms of needing to be "one-up" on other people. I was stuck on Step Seven with the irony that lack of humility was the defect, so asking "humbly" was a catch-22. Part of my insight was that I mattered to my group even when I intentionally put myself "one-down" by staying silent in meetings.

A friend had the opposite problem. She had been painfully abused and neglected as a child and grew up with the subconscious belief that she was worthless. Consequently, she habitually allowed herself to be mistreated, even sought out bad treatment, and contributed by her own unwise actions.

She saw herself as one-down from everybody and not deserving of decent treatment or a good life. With support from a good sponsor, a strong home group, and some professional help, she began to see her reality more clearly. A good Fourth Step led her to see her good qualities and her strengths. She began to see how her false beliefs about herself connected to her unwise behavior patterns. Her shortcomings were failures to believe strongly enough in herself and her self-worth. For her, when she came to Step Seven, humble meant seeing her positive qualities.

My friend says she found relief in seeing her own value. She said, "It feels good to know I can do things, that I'm okay." I, too, found relief in being right-sized. Humility means I needn't struggle to show I am one-up, and I needn't pretend to feel one-down. Being right-sized is comfortable.

Summarizing Step Seven

Step Seven says, Humbly asked Him to remove our shortcomings Here's what I have ended up with after struggling with that Step.

- Knowing about my defects of character isn't enough to be rid of them.
- Noticing when I know better and doing it wrong any way (shortcoming) is a sign of progress.
- Humility is a huge relief.

So, I need a realistic view of myself, a proper understanding of my relationship to my Higher Power, and a healthy appreciation of my relationship to you and every human being. Then I can ask for help on choices to prevent taking actions I know to be unwise.

My Step Six experiences didn't happen just once. In fact, they continue as I continue on my spiritual path. I become "entirely ready" on different issues and varying depths as I keep paying attention to the day-to-day events in my life. As I become aware of my shortcomings, I meditate and pray, ponder and contemplate. Sometimes I think I have unraveled a behavior and found one of the cracks in the basement of my mind, and I can pray for clarity about a mis- taken belief. Sometimes I'm still not sure about the mistaken belief, but I can pray for help in controlling the unwise behavior and exposing the false belief.

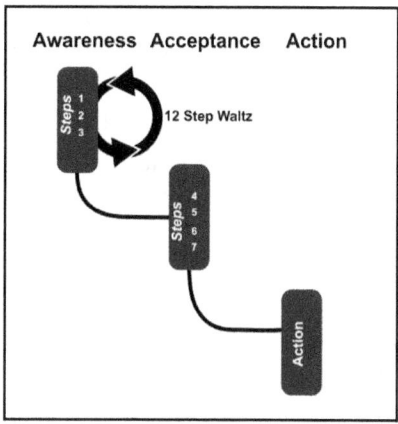

This is the work of Step Seven. I know my Higher Power has responded when I begin to be aware of the pain of unwise choices and appreciate (accept) the connection between that pain and a wrong belief. Eventually, I see shortcomings fade and gradually disappear from my life.

When I began to see my life being reshaped, I could confidently move on to Step Eight.

Getting The Feel Of A New Life

STEPS ONE, TWO, AND THREE HELPED ME get a grip on reality. Once I got some real grounding about the universe I was actually living in rather than the universe that I ad imagined in my denial, I could work Steps Four and Five and assemble a lot of information about my reality. With all that information, I got a chance in Steps Six and Seven to recommit to taking the actions necessary for a better life. These Steps got me to Awareness, Acceptance, and inward-facing Action in a spiritual universe.

In Steps Eight and Nine, I get to do things that make it possible to live comfortably with my new understanding of myself and reality. I take my inward-facing Action and point it outward toward all my past relationships.

Step Eight

Made a list of all persons we had harmed, and became willing to make amends to them all.

In Step Eight, with my Higher Power's help, I start to take actions that will change my life permanently for the better. In Steps Six and Seven, I committed to this new life. In Step Eight, I start to make recovery happen.

What does recovery feel like? On a good day in recovery, I feel confident, optimistic, a little mischievous. I feel comfortable being me. I act quickly to help when I see others struggling or in need of a boost. I do little things to improve my surroundings, my neighborhood, or my society. Some days I have more of this feeling, some days less. The longer I am in recovery, the more a good day feels normal, and a normal day feels good.

I've heard in the rooms, "Come to meetings to feel better; to get better, do the Steps." All the work I did from Step One through Step Seven put me on a path to a more

Getting the Feel of a New Life (Steps 8, 9)

real, better informed, healthier life. And it doesn't stop. The Twelve Step waltz keeps on as I encounter, then accept, then give up control of uncontrollable things. The cycle of becoming aware of my shortcomings and digging into the underlying mistaken beliefs keeps happening. The feelings that come with these cycles aren't necessarily pleasant; I still don't enjoy uncovering my imperfections, but when I see progress, it feels good.

All the Step work so far was essential, but there's more to a good life than improving the internals of my mind. I also had to get straight with the people in my life that my unwise choices have injured. I didn't give up inward observation (that's a permanent feature of my good life). Still, much of what I uncovered in the first few years of my program raised uncomfortable memories of past actions and decisions that I regretted. Hence Step Eight.

Step Eight starts small; I make a list. And once more, being careful about what the words mean, I can get useful insights. With this Step, I needed to be careful about the meaning of "harmed."

Back in Step Five, we were careful about the meaning of "wrongs" and restated Step Five to say "... the exact nature of our unwise choices and actions and the unwanted consequences that resulted." Unwise actions led to unwanted consequences of various kinds. Some were disappointments, and some were failures. The focus in Step Eight is on the unwanted consequences that harmed people.

In A.A., there has been a focus on what members have done to other people. The chaos of the active disease often creates a trail of damage to relationships and often damage to property, businesses, or even strangers. In Al-Anon, we also address these kinds of harm, but we are likely as well to pay attention to the harms we have done to ourselves.

My Al-Anon sponsor gently reminded me that among the victims of my unwise choices, I might have suffered as much or more than others. I was told, "Put your name on the top of the list."

Harms, damage, negative impacts — that's what this Step asks us to think about. If I have harmed someone, that

page 83

person goes on the list. Even though the Step says "people," sometimes I might feel that I acted unwisely with a non-person, and I'd feel better if I got that off my chest. If some unwise action caused some harm I can't identify to a specific person (did I cheat on my taxes?), it may be appropriate to add that to the list.

For the most part, making the list felt pretty good to me. It was as if getting the guilty memories out of my head and onto some paper was progress. When I started my personal Eighth Step, for example, I remembered that there was a dog who had been the unwitting victim of my behavior. So the dog went on the list.

On the other hand, some of the memories were very sensitive, and I didn't want to look too closely. For example, the first time through the harm I caused my children was just too painful, and it stayed covered up in denial for another year.

The Step says, "made a list," and the list can be pretty simple, just names, but I think it's helpful to add a couple more columns like this.

Who I harmed	What happened	Possible Amends

Of course, the very painful people and the incidents of harm may be hard to face. I think sketchy may be all right for a while. I'm recommending the "what happened" column because we don't always clearly know what the harm was or even if harm was involved.

For instance, when I was about ten, I took swimming lessons at the local college. The instructor announced that there would be an "open" class where we could invite a parent or friend to join in. I begged my father to come to the class with me, and finally, he agreed even though it meant his leaving work early.

We arrived at the pool swimsuits, towels, and all to discover I had gotten the date wrong, and the open swim was

Getting the Feel of a New Life (Steps 8, 9)

the next week. I was hugely embarrassed and felt that my dad must be similarly embarrassed (although the instructors insisted my dad join in, and he seemed to have a good time).

I carried the guilt of this mistaken invitation to my father for many years, and when I finally dared to recall the incident with him and apologize, he couldn't remember it at all. Without that conversation, I might have put this on my list, but no harm had actually been done.

Sometimes there are unwanted outcomes, but there's no one at fault. My action may have had nothing to do with the damage someone else suffered. Sometimes stuff just happens. To assure I'm not taking responsibility for damage that isn't mine, it's useful to go over the list with a sponsor or trusted friend. Just explaining my thinking can give some perspective, and another person's view is always helpful, especially in highly charged emotional situations.

Step Eight is not where I begin to make amends, but it's nearly impossible to make this list without looking beyond the harms to the amends I will eventually make. I think it's useful to start that thinking during Step Eight. I consider such thinking ahead to be an obvious, unavoidable part of "[becoming] willing to make amends to them all."

The exact form of the amends doesn't have to be clear at this point. I may have a tentative idea of the amends based on my present perspective. Yet, as time goes on, understanding, wisdom, and compassion grow. Perhaps my perspective will change. So consider the details just a starting point.

Becoming "willing to make amends" is like "were entirely ready" — it's a state of being, not an action. Members often advise that we can take the "willing" part a bit at a time. The literature suggests that we can split our Eighth Step list into degrees of willingness: willing to make amends now, may become ready to make amends sometime in the future, and Never-ever, no way will I make amends to that person. (Paths to Recovery p.82 and How Al-Anon Works p.59) Often the table looks like this.

Ready to make these	Who I harmed	What happened	Possible Amends
May make these	Who I harmed	What happened	Possible Amends
Never make these	Who I harmed	What happened	Possible Amends

As we work Step Nine, experience affects willingness. Each good experience makes it easier to contemplate and "become willing" to make additional amends. Maybe feedback we get while making Ninth Step amends might change our understanding of the events in our lives and our part in them. The list and its details can change as we mature in recovery.

Summarizing Step Eight

Step Eight says, Made a list of all persons we had harmed, and became willing to make amends to them all. Here's what I've concluded about the Step.

- Making a list is easy, but getting the proper names on it is a bit challenging.
- It's helpful to be specific about the harms.
- I needed to put myself on the list.
- Harms I did myself needed to be understood, and the amends to myself needed to be carefully considered.
- Willingness can't be forced, but it can be nurtured.
- Steps Eight and Nine work together, and progress is incremental.

This tentative, incremental approach to Step Eight means taking Steps Eight and Nine as an interacting set. So let's take a look at Step Nine to see how that works.

Step Nine

Made direct amends to such people wherever possible, except when to do so would injure them or others.

Step Eight had us make a list of those we had harmed and become ready to make amends. If I'm not prepared to make amends to everyone on the list, the wisdom of the program urges me to make amends I am ready for and trust that new experience and the help of my Higher Power will move people up my list from "never" to "maybe" and from "maybe" to "ready."

In Step Nine, the focus shifts to precisely what is involved in making amends. But, again, questions arise as I contemplate the practical actions I have committed to taking.

- Is "sorry" enough?
- Can I undo the harm I've caused?
- What can I do to repair what I've broken or to compensate for the harm?

A difficult fact is that situations, harms, and amends are all unique, and I have to call on sound judgment and faith as I make case-by-case decisions. However, the welcome fact is that having come this far in the Steps, I have a better grasp on reality, a more robust support network for counsel, example, and advice, and a growing practical faith that I can rely on.

By Step Nine, I am better prepared to understand the likely consequences of my actions clearly. In addition, I have a sponsor, program friends, and a community from which to draw support. And, I have a God of my understanding to lend me serenity, courage, and wisdom as I plan and carry out these anxiety-prone and often uncomfortable tasks.

A personal experience

I would never have been involved in this business venture except for the boss. First, he asked me to help as a consultant. Then he asked me to join as a founder. He was the boss, the leader, and the supposed expert entrepreneur. At first, there were just four of us; there was a marketing guy, a fellow with some money, the boss, and me. Four years later, it was a growing venture business with a good idea and dozens of employees depending on us.

My job was operations and technology, and we were ahead of schedule and breaking new ground every day. But money was running out. Marketing was failing, and sales were more than a year behind schedule. Worse thing, the boss was locked away in his office, depressed and distracted.

At management meetings, I started complaining, then started criticizing, finally getting nasty with the other partners. Of course, I was right, wasn't I, because I had to be perfect. I was fearful, angry, and blaming. One thing led to another—a big blow-up. I was fired.

Years later, after the company had failed, I was working Steps Eight and Nine, and I had amends to make to both the boss and the marketing partner. I had done harm. In responding to the business crisis, I had been a know-it-all instead of a partner. I had failed to improve the situation, the problems just got worse, and through my attitude, I became such an irritant they finally decided to throw me out. Perhaps, I could have helped with wiser choices and, if not, would at least have been a better friend and partner.

I invited the marketing guy to lunch. After four years, he was surprised but accepted. I made my amends, and he said, "Yeah, those were tough times. I appreciate your saying you had a part. I guess we all did." So we parted, if not as friends, at least without hostility.

The boss had moved away, but I managed a visit to his new city and made my amends to him in a similar way. He responded in a snarky tone, "Thanks for at last admitting you were wrong. You really helped destroy a pretty good company." Evidently, he thought he had had no part in the company's failure.

Same harm, same amends, two very different responses.

There is not a single pattern for amends

It's not possible to generalize about making amends because "harms" come in such a variety. For example, perhaps I said something in anger or ignorance that destroyed a friendship. I may have harmed my friend; certainly, I broke the friendship, and (because it was on my conscience) undoubtedly, I was harmed. However, my objective is to clear my side of the street, not to resurrect the friendship.

I apologize for my unwise action. It is not necessary to explain at great length my situation at the time or the failures that caused my thoughtless action. If the result is a restored friendship, I am pleased with this extra benefit. Even if my ex-friend is cool or rejects my apology, I have done my part and can move on with guilt removed.

Perhaps I have done weightier harm, truly injured someone emotionally, financially, or even physically. Such situations require substantial and sometimes very difficult amends. It is not enough to say, "I'm sorry." The necessary action to repair the harm may be obvious — repay the borrowed money, replace the broken keepsake, give the credit due — or the action may require that I ask the person I have harmed how I can compensate for the damage done.

Each amends in Step Nine is a different challenge that helps us draw on our faith and clarity. Again, the Twelve Step literature can help us with some examples.

- One recovering A.A. member had lied about a business transaction, and an innocent party had been ruined financially and socially. The member finally decided that his amends required public admission of the harm he had caused. He rose in church on Sunday and explained the harm and his remorse. (A.A. Big Book p.80)
- A woman in Al-Anon recovery decided that the best way to make amends to her parents was to become the kind of daughter they deserved, making many smaller amends whenever she'd visit. (Paths to Recovery p.94)

- One Al-Anon realized she had been a thief all her life with too many past victims to find and reimburse. She made a cash donation to a charity and found herself in the middle of a miracle. (How Al-Anon Works pp. 202-203)
- An Al-Anon wanted to make amends to her Father but avoided it with trepidation for years. One day when they were alone together in a quiet place, her amends seemed to pore out of her without planning, effort, or fear. (Paths to Recovery p.95)
- Another long-term Al-Anon wasn't ever able to express her amends to her father directly but noticed that he was happiest when he was with his grandchildren, and she made a special effort as long as he lived to make visits possible. (Paths to Recovery p.97)
- Another member decided that the best amends she could make to herself was to change the relationships with her alcoholic family for the better by making choices that supported her serenity and self-respect. (Hope For Today p.120)
- One woman learned what making amends looks like and how it can be done by receiving a surprise from another Al-Anon who made amends to her. (Hope For Today p.259)
- A man struggled with himself but eventually found a way to begin understanding, forgiving, and finally making amends even though his abusive alcoholic father was long dead. (Hope For Today p.296)
- An adult child of an alcoholic family discovered her part in the family chaos and made a plan to use the slogan "Let it begin with me" to help her direct amends to her parents. (Hope For Today p.296)
- A woman said, "I make amends to myself by changing how I treat myself now and serving others, things that I was unable to do for myself when I was in their situation." (How Al-Anon Works p.179)

A little more personal experience

- I could never make direct amends to one of the essential people on my list because she died before I could read her the letter of amends I had written.
- In my Fourth Step, I had to admit that I had abused a small white dog in my pre-recovery anger. Often it had been easier to holler at the dog than deal with the alcoholic. So I put the dog on my Eighth Step list and made the best amends I could by playing the dog's favorite tugging game and taking her for her favorite walks for the rest of her life. The program calls this a living amends.
- I would have made an amends to a friend who had died years ago, but it was too late. Step Nine led me to make living amends by working hard at supporting and loving a different friend who was dying.
- After I had done several amends from my list, I wrote a very candid self-addressed letter apologizing for the harms I had inflicted on myself and promising to do better in the future. Eventually, I wrote another letter of forgiveness to myself.

Summarizing Step Nine

Step Nine says, Made direct amends to such people wherever possible, except when to do so would injure them or others. Here's how I sum up what I've learned about the Step.

- Making amends is very personal and very specific to the nature of the harm and the people involved.
- "Sorry" is not enough; sorry may not even be appropriate.
- Amends are not necessarily received graciously. Obtaining forgiveness is not the purpose, and it may not be forthcoming.

The best practical advice for the Al-Anon approach to Step Nine I have found says:

> *"We cannot undo what has been done ... There are many ways to make amends ... Prayer and meditation [as well as friends, sponsors] are also illuminating ... Emphasis of this Step is on facing those we have harmed and setting the record straight ... With*

this Step we have the opportunity to choose the kind of person we would like to become ... We demonstrate that we wish to be fair, honest, and mature ... and set ourselves free." (How Al-Anon Works pp. 59-61)

Grooving The Swing

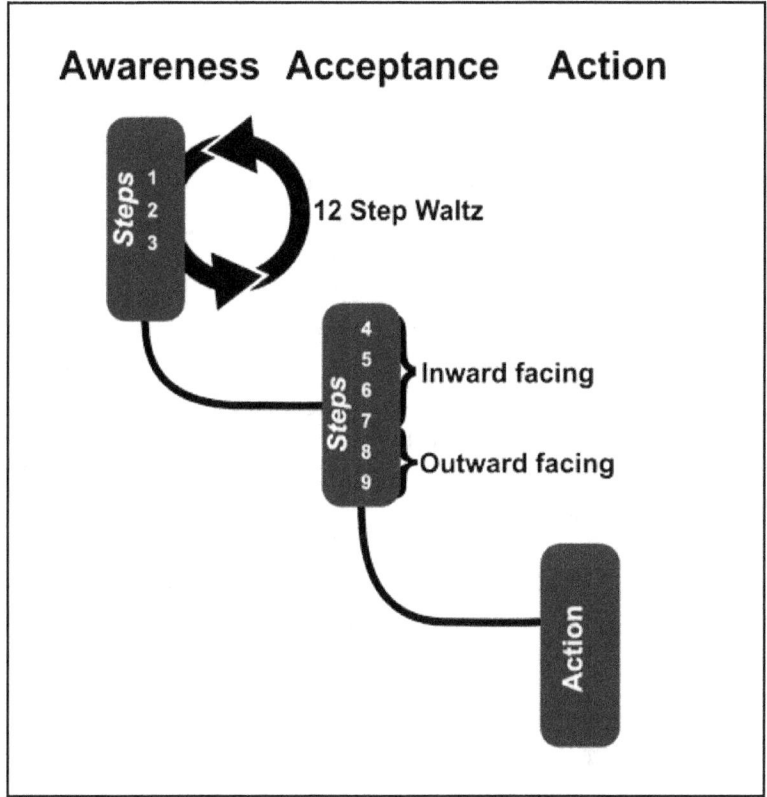

THE GOLF INSTRUCTOR OR THE BATTING COACH will tell me to repeat the correct motion repeatedly until my body and subconscious establish the habit of doing it right. They call it "grooving the swing." I think about the last three Steps similarly. We do the last few Steps over and over until they become a habit in a new life of sanity.

Once more, we are back to the three As (Awareness, Acceptance, and Action).

- My Higher Power and I used Steps One, Two, and Three to build awareness of the reality in which I live. As a result, I began to crack through the shell of denial and resentment that blocked me from the good life I want.
- Steps Four and Five helped me build a realistic picture of myself and accept my particular mix of wise and unwise actions.
- In Steps Six and Seven, I extended Acceptance to the unique place I hold in the universe. But, most important, I accepted my relationship to my Higher Power and how the God of my understanding could shape me and build me into the person I want to be.
- In Steps Eight and Nine, inward-facing action shifted to outward-facing. I took specific actions to clear my side of the street and experienced the joy and freedom of living in the sunlight of the spirit.

In the three or four years while I was doing the first nine Steps, my life changed. My relationship with the last active alcoholic in my life was finally over, a painful drama to the end. Then, finally, the peacefulness was like a warm blanket on a cold night.

I gave up financial competitiveness and settled into a comfortable, modest late-career doing work I value and enjoy. I seem to spend less and less effort shaping the image other people have of me. Instead, I spend more time in introspection, marveling at the complexity and intricacy of the one human mind I can examine from the inside. People seem to like me better.

The changes have been good ones, and I want to keep them. That's what the last three Steps are about. Sometimes, we call Steps Ten, Eleven, and Twelve "maintenance Steps," but I don't think that gives them enough credit. I prefer to think of my recovery from Step One to Step Nine as just a beginning, not a place to settle and maintain.

The last three Steps are actions about growing, not stopping.

Step Ten
Continued to take personal inventory and when we were wrong promptly admitted it.

Okay, we know what a personal inventory is; we did a searching and fearless one in Step Four. Do I have to do Step Four over again in Step Ten? Probably not. Personally, I learned a lot about myself in Step Four, and my path has taken me back a couple of times to do a few more Fourth Steps, but I don't think that's what Step Ten is about.

What is Step Ten about?

First, note that the "searching and fearless [and] moral" inventory of Step Four is generalized to a "personal" inventory in Step Ten. This is an acknowledgment that now I have nothing to fear from examining my behavior, and, now, since I have a lot of experience, I don't have so much searching to do. Of course, the "moral" nature of the inventory hasn't gone away, but it has been extended to a broader examination of everything I do.

I make choices every minute. I can't help it. The universe won't let me stand still, but it's up to me which direction I take and what I do. Step Ten is about helping me make better choices.

Step Ten is a bridge

It's often said of the Twelve Steps, "This is a simple program," and, of course, that's true, but knowing that it works, while joyful, leaves me asking: how does it work?

In our Twelve Step work, we get at our fundamental nature indirectly. We experience changes in our minds' basements, and we practice behaviors that serve us better, but we leave the theory to be implied. We usually don't ask how we got screwed up and, when we experience the Twelve Step miracle, we typically don't ask how we got so un-screwed up. What if we did ask those questions? What is going on that makes my life better?

I believe we have to spend time with spiritual practices and projects for them to do their work. I see the Steps as a framework for learning how to pursue a spiritual path, and my program is more discovery than recovery. So it's fair to ask: is there a learning curve for this stuff? What exactly is happening?

I have outlined a theory of the Twelve Steps with the big picture view as the three As. Awareness develops in the first three Steps. Acceptance is the purpose of Steps Four through Nine. Now, in the last three Steps, it's all about Action. Step Ten is the bridge by which I take the experiences and new learning from the first nine Steps and put it all to work, helping me make wiser decisions and take healthier actions. These are profound changes, and I want to understand how such vital changes happen.

How change happens

Everything in the universe has a place, an energy, and everything is changing. But click, in the next instant, everything has a new place, new energy, and still is changing. Click. Click. Click. I find this enormous, endless change a little intimidating. I imagine that if my human mind could appreciate the immensity of what is actually happening in the universe, it would be terrifying ... but wonderful!

If I took a picture of the entire universe at each instant and compared it to the immediately previous image and then again and again back through the earlier pictures, I could watch the universe and see how everything got to be the way it is. If I looked back through the pictures, I could see the history of the universe all the way back to the Big Bang (another elegant idea too big for my mind to really hold).

Looking back through the pictures, I would never see sudden jumps or gaps. A tree grows and dies and disappears but never jumps from the backyard to the front. So even though I can't know exactly what the next picture will be, I do know that it will be pretty much like the last. Changes will take place, but only those changes which are possible. Leaves will fall, but they won't suddenly become birds.

Grooving the Swing (Steps 10, 11, 12)

There are infinite possible next pictures, and which image will be selected is genuinely unknowable. Still, I can be sure that it will emerge from one of the possible futures, the adjacent (but unknowable) possible.

Of course, you and I are not casual observers of this constant change. We don't just watch the story; we are also writing it. Every day we step into the unknown possible. We are guided by our individual collection of beliefs, values, principles, and mental models. I usually call this collection of cognitive tools a mindset, but I could just as easily and correctly call it my faith.

Paying attention leads to better choices

As I worked the program, my faith grew and changed. I no longer felt alone in the restless, unpredictable, inescapable universe. Instead, I was cared for by a power greater than myself in a way I didn't understand, but the comfort I got from that care made me feel safe. When I could make conscious contact with the source of that care, the feeling was joy.

I started relying on my new faith, and my life got better, but the old beliefs and drives, the ones I call defects of character, didn't disappear. For example, the need to be perfect still reaches out from the basement all the time, but I'm a lot less anxious and obnoxious about it. I notice this feeling now and often can stop unwise words that still form in my mind from falling out my mouth. In my nightly prayers, I give thanks for this self-knowledge and self-control.

The daily inventory of the Tenth Step just means paying attention to my actions and my motivations. As long as I'm acting according to my faith, I'm doing the best I can. If I note that I have acted based on an old defect, I get clarity about the shortcoming, and I admit it. I let the information soak in.

Engineers will see this as a simple feedback loop. For example, it starts like this:

> *When my neighbor told me she didn't have house plants because they took all the oxygen out of the air, I couldn't resist explaining basic plant biology to her.*

As you can imagine, she wasn't at all grateful. Even while I explained photosynthesis in my best academic tone, I could feel that I was making a mistake. I was both showing off to my neighbor and trying to control her behavior. I was playing a role that I felt comfortable in, one-up.

That night at prayer-time, I reviewed that incident with my Higher Power. I recalled the uncomfortable moment, and I reviewed my part. That was Awareness. I recognized my behavior was motivated by pride and the old defects of character. I noted the shortcoming and admitted that I had been wrong. That's Acceptance.

Awareness, Acceptance, and then the Action: I sought my Higher Power's help ... "God, if it's your will, in situations like this, please place your hand over my mouth."

The example is about a shortcoming but let's note that Step Ten isn't just about defects of character and shortcomings.

You'll agree, I think, that it's generally helpful to pay attention to the outcomes of our actions and, if something didn't work, to try to figure out what went wrong. For example, did I believe something that wasn't true? Was my mental model of the situation inadequate or defective? How confident am I of the perceptions and conclusions on which I based my actions and decisions? If any of these were weak, fuzzy, or wrong, I should admit it promptly — that is, let it into my consciousness — so that my future choices can be wiser. This kind of conscious learning experience drives detailed changes in my mindset and cleans up the basement of my mind.

I do this Step in the evening with a gratitude prayer like this, "Thank you, God, for taking care of me today, giving me a good day, and keeping me safe." If I consciously focus on the gratitude for the day I have lived, I seem automatically to review the day's events — positive and negative — and screen them for wrongs. Holding the gratitude in the forefront of my mind takes the sting out of mistakes I've made so that I can see them as learning opportunities.

Step Ten is not a one-shot deal. Instead, it's a helpful habit to adopt for everyday use, and it's not the only one.

Maybe you're wondering how long do I have to do the Steps? The answer I offer in the following few paragraphs has to do with the nature of the Steps and the good life we are promised when we have done them.

Being human sometimes gets in the way

My program work has convinced me that our evolution, our biology, and our culture mold our minds in a uniquely human way. And, while this mindset serves us well as a species seeking to survive, it serves us poorly as beings seeking to live healthy, satisfying lives. Thus, it seems that an essential part of a spiritual path is discovering the true nature of life as a human being.

Things that make me human make a spiritual life difficult. I am designed to deal with what I see, react out of my basic instincts, and build a survival mindset from everyday experience. Evolution and natural selection created an animal sufficiently complex to maintain the glow of consciousness and conscience. But, the animal parts interfere when I try to emerge into the sunlight of the spirit. Desire, anger, and fear are barriers to conscious contact with my Higher Power.

This insight is gratifying to the extent that it explains why the complexities of modern life seem to be a constant source of stress and confusion. Yet, on the other hand, the reality is frustrating. I like understanding things. My rational mind has been my best tool all my life. What an irony to discover that, in critical ways, it has also been my biggest obstacle!

No matter what I believe about the connection between the brain, mind, and spirit, I must recognize that the brain does essential things for me. So I need to pay attention to some of the implications of my physical being. It always takes time and usually repeated stimulation to make brain cells grow, change, or reroute. The advertising industry says I have to see an ad 3.5 times before I'll remember the product. It's no surprise that I will have to see unwise behavior more than once to recognize it, let my brain reroute a whole decision-making process, and decide to do something else.

Change takes time

There is no doubt that my brain's components for remembering, projecting, reasoning, and emoting have a physiological basis, neurons, axons, dendrites, electrical and chemical signaling, etc. For my spiritual path to lead to profound changes in my behavior, it seems inevitable that there will have to be changes in my brain physiology. Is it any surprise that healing the cracks in my soul takes time, effort, and repetition? While doing the Steps, I re-experience my life and expose my mind's workings and, as the thoughts and fears of my subconscious are examined in the light of the spirit, circuits in my brain gradually rewire themselves. Experience by experience, I relearn my way into healthier behavior.

That's how change happens in my mind, but it isn't easy, and it isn't quick. And, of course, as soon as I understand my character defects, I want them gone... right now! At first, my impatience was almost painful. As the years have passed, though, and I have seen change, slow as it is, actually happens, I find it easier to tolerate my Higher Power's leisurely pace. Of course, I don't like being imperfect, but I have learned to be more tolerant of my shortcomings, making life more pleasant for me and people close to me.

I wish to live skillfully in a way that sets aside my animal nature to experience reality's spiritual dimension. Living unwisely comes naturally; I didn't have to practice anger or fear. Living skillfully, on the other hand, requires learning, practice, and experience.

A spiritual path consists of the lessons, exercises, and events that lead me to a more skillful life. If I reach for a metaphor, I might say that my spiritual path is the chisel, and I am the stone. Stones do not change by themselves, and I don't take the Steps of my path spontaneously. My Higher Power is the sculptor. The positive dynamics of the spiritual universe impel my steps.

But feeling better isn't quite the same as being better. Being better takes time. It takes time because understanding and believing new things, while necessary, isn't enough; I have to do something to change for the better.

Healthy change requires paying attention

I'm sure you've heard the advice, "Go with the flow." That is, don't struggle against reality. Good advice as far as it goes, but maybe too simplistic to provide much understanding. Life does not proceed from one moment to the next like a bit of flotsam drifting down a stream.

Each of us chooses the next instant of life in a complex ballet of selection and synthesis. A storm of sense-data bombards us. We filter and select from the sense-data based on a combination of instinct, habit, and attention. The sense data is interpreted and understood by a consciousness that connects the last moment with the present moment, weaving a personal history from memory, mental models, and momentary experience. Understood in this way, we can see how a spiritual path leads to a healthier life.

If we give our attention to this moment's sense-data by consciously staying in the moment, clarity reveals real choices. When we clear our conscious and subconscious minds of denial, attachment, and character defects, it's possible to select the next moment of our lives more wisely. But, of course, even focusing on the wrong data and filtering it through error, we will choose from the adjacent possible. But with such a careless choice, we should expect to suffer confusion and frustration. Flowing is okay, but it's no substitute for paying attention.

Are the Steps a spiritual path?

It seems to me that a spiritual path is a transformation in which I am reprogramming my subconscious mind. The Twelve Steps have had an important place in that transformation, but I don't think that's the whole story.

Not a newbie any more

When I was new in the program, I thought it made sense

that the Twelve Steps was a way of life, a permanent commitment to health supported by a sympathetic and understanding community. I thought the Steps were all I needed to heal my wounds, lift my spirits, and find serenity. I know many people who say that they are lifers; they will always have an Al-Anon program and will be active in the fellowship for as long as they live. For many of us, this decision is precisely and resoundingly the right one. But maybe not for all of us.

I have great enthusiasm, respect, and gratitude for the Twelve Steps, but now I don't see the Steps as a path. I see them as a recipe for making a spiritual journey, not the journey itself. The genius of Twelve Step programs is their flexibility to serve a broad range of minds and hearts. It's my pace, my understanding, my decision, my spiritual awakening. "Having had a spiritual awakening," as it says in Step Twelve, I continue my path and my practice.

For me, the whole idea of a spiritual path was a significant change. At first, I didn't get it, and I didn't want it. I kept coming back, though, because I felt better at the end of each Twelve Step experience than at the beginning. Like being translated into a different time and place, some things were familiar, some were uncomfortable, and a lot was hard to swallow, but I was in enough pain to close my eyes and gulp the experience down.

After years on the path, I think I understand some of what happened to me. The shared experiences — meetings, ceremonies, sponsorship, intimate conversation, literature, and service — taken together for long enough, form a context in which my mind is reformed. The new vocabulary and concepts gradually merge into a new understanding of reality. The accumulation of other people's stories provides memories while I am accumulating my own.

Frankly, some days it's easier to just relax into my old habits, but there's something deeply compelling about the search for a better life, and I don't seem to be able to stay away from the work for very long. New mental models and new experiences change me.

That's the point of the whole program — change — especially Step Ten which I paraphrase as "Pay attention!"

How do I know what spiritual work to do?

When I read, listen, or observe, I am engaging in a rational activity, one of the things that humans are good at. However, spiritual awareness, spiritual awakening, and spiritual action occur in a realm of human experience that rationality does not serve well. No matter how carefully or how often I think through the Twelve Steps, there is no sense of "being done." No matter how logically I understand, no matter how articulately I explain, no matter how great my Twelve Step scholarship, my goal of a good life may still elude me. The studying I do loads me up with information and, perhaps, inspiration, but spiritual growth requires some other process.

The rationality I use to understand spiritual teaching prepares the ground, but spiritual growth requires actions, and the actions are the spiritual tools. So I am urged by some to meditate, by others to pray unceasingly, and by others to do service work.

Self-awareness is the great gift of being human, the foundation of free will. Sadly the gift covers my spiritual eyes and makes it hard for me to see that I already stand in the sunlight of the spirit. It seems that a common feature of spiritual tools is that they work to get my rational mind out of the way.

I believe that it is beneficial to look beyond the Twelve Step literature and the Twelve Step program to appreciate the true nature of a spiritual life. The great religions of the world and the great enduring philosophical conversations have a wealth of information about the spiritual life, and, in many profound ways, they agree. Almost without exception, the sages and saints encourage me to pray, meditate, and study They urge self-examination, gratitude, and generosity in action. These, they say, are the elements of a good spiritual workout. Different traditions and different teachers suggest different details, and some insist that their details are the only ones that work. With due respect to those who claim exclusivity, I doubt it.

I believe there is no single path to closeness with my Higher Power. I believe that such intimacy is already and always present. My spiritual development depends on actions that make me aware of that closeness. I don't follow a path to the sunlight of the spirit; I open my eyes.

All of the change I have experienced in my path has been peeling away layer after layer of mindset defenses that inhibit connection to the spiritual dimension of reality which, I have come to believe, is where sanity has always been.

The great genius of the Twelve Steps

I believe that the profound genius, enormous power, and transcendent wisdom of our Twelve Step programs are, in large part, the result of what is left out. The Steps give us what we need, each in our own way, to find a spiritual path, but do it in a way that is permissive, never coercive. We say the program is spiritual-not-religious and it is, but the fundamental problems which philosophy and religion address do not go away.

Our Twelve Step programs don't answer many of the great questions, but through the Steps we heal enough so that we can seek our answers in joy instead of despair, in health rather than sickness, and in community rather than isolation.

Some Twelve Steppers will be happy to argue that the Steps, the A.A. Big Book, a meeting, and a Higher Power are all you need for recovery. They like to say, "This is a simple program. Thinking is what got us into this mess in the first place!" I'd never argue with them, but I will say to you that I think reality is bigger than that.

Beyond the Steps

Al-Anon members sometimes summarize the program as simply, mind your own business and get a life. But, for me, I add another thought, pay attention!

Socrates told us the unexamined life is not worth living. My experience is that the unexamined life is a foul swamp of ignorance. Getting out of the swamp requires me to challenge what I believe and what I feel and question what I think I know. This sort of self-examination doesn't happen by accident and, while the Steps have been my life-savers in the swamp, more attention, more examination, and more varied perspectives have always helped me.

At its foundation, a Twelve Step program leads to recovery and, though recovery can be the beginning of a new spiritual way of life, it isn't a complete spiritual path. So it's a mistake, I think, for those of us who have found recovery in the Steps to narrow our thinking to this program, this program exclusively, or this program forever.

A spiritual awakening is bigger than that ... way bigger!

Rarely in all the recovery literature will you find explicit rules. There are no commandments, and there is nothing about moral error or sin. Indeed, there is occasional advice and lots of suggestions, but there is no explanation of what it means to have a good life.

We get to make our own definitions and descriptions. We learn we can be restored to sanity, and we understand that sanity includes having a better life, but the program leaves the details to me. I get to decide what actions I will take to be a good person, a good citizen, and live that better life.

What is the good life like?

We often say Twelve Step recovery means "getting a life," as if the suffering that brought us to a program wasn't living. Well, it certainly wasn't good living. So it makes sense that if I want a good life, I ought to say what a good life is.

In the Al-Anon rooms, I've heard the expression "happy, joyous, and free." I guess that's the feeling to aim for, but to me, this phrase seems too goody-goody, too much Pollyanna. Life, especially a good life, is a lot more complicated.

Some philosophers have suggested that the object of a good life is happiness defined in a particular way. The kind of happiness they mean isn't *great-party-last-night* happiness. Instead, it's more a *be-all-you-can-be* kind of happiness. That kind of happiness depends on the sort of person I am and how I am connected to you and the universe. My spiritual path gives me clues about both. The more I've learned about me — about how I relate to the seen and unseen universe, and about loving you, the more wisdom and compassion I acquire — the better my life becomes.

Following the path is a good life. Life becomes good because my mind is bent, folded, cajoled, and coaxed into a wiser, more compassionate, more loving shape. Denial is chipped away, and resentment abandoned. In short, I grow up; I mature.

- Maturity and wisdom are values we seek in recovery and along our spiritual path. It's clear when we're dealing with immaturity, but it isn't always clear what maturity and wisdom are, so here is a summary of what I mean by maturity and how wisdom behaves:
- Maturity comes from understanding: clarity about the nature of reality and a firm grasp of the obvious. Wisdom doesn't believe absurdities.
- Maturity brings discernment: we can distinguish real from unreal, healthy from unhealthy, and wise from unwise. Wisdom doesn't confuse right and wrong.
- Maturity embodies character: compassion and wisdom combine with strength and courage. Wisdom forsakes indifference, illuminates ignorance, and manages fear.
- Maturity and wisdom take responsibility: I own my stuff. So don't shirk, shrink, shift, or squirm.
- Maturity acts with moderation: the extreme, the radical, and the absolute are put aside. Wisdom avoids over-reaction, extremism, and fundamentalism.
- Maturity has balance: ascetics to the left, gluttons to the right, the mature path down the middle. Wisdom doesn't wallow in indulgence, flaunt abstinence, or bolt from one to the other.

I've heard it said that addicts only mature during those days and weeks when they are sober, drunk-time and high-time, I'm told, are lost growth opportunities. I'd add that time spent obsessing in the future or the past is lost time even if I'm sober. Spiritual growth and maturity grow one present moment at a time. Right here, right now, I know I grow.

Summarizing Step Ten

Step Ten says, Continued to take personal inventory and when we were wrong promptly admitted it. Here are essential thoughts about the Step.

- Do this Step regularly and often.
- I'm not punishing or judging myself; I'm paying attention.
- It's not just about unwise behavior; it's about making wise behavior wiser.
- I try to remember it's my inventory, not someone else's.
- I need to be gentle and patient with myself.
- Paying attention to my behavior helps me minimize judging and gossiping.
- Step Ten puts the program to work and takes my thinking beyond the Steps.

Growing into maturity is part of living a good life. My spiritual path is the everyday work I do to grow, gain, and keep my maturity. Step Ten is a check I take every day to see how well I'm doing.

Step Eleven

Sought through prayer and meditation to improve our conscious contact with God as we understood Him, praying only for knowledge of His will for us and the power to carry that out.

This Step is extremely rich in concepts that can confuse me. For instance:

- What exactly are prayer and meditation? Are they different? When I want to pray or meditate, how do I do it?

- What does conscious contact with God feel like? Can that happen to me?
- Why am I "[seeking] to improve [it]" instead of just improving it?
- Why should my prayers be restricted to these specific types of prayer?
- How will I experience knowing God's will? What will the "power" feel like?

We'll take a shot at answering these as we go along in this section, but let's start with digging into what this Step is really all about.

Step Eleven basic concept

All my actions in my Twelve Step program have nudged me in the direction of my Higher Power. It went like this: admitted the possibility in Step Two; made a decision in Step Three; looked inside in Step Four; and shared my self-discovery with my Higher Power in Step Five. Then I became ready for my Higher Power to change me in Step Six and asked for specific changes in Step Seven. Finally, Steps Eight and Nine were taken to turn my face to the sunlight of the spirit.

In the growth Steps, I nurture the connection I have with my Higher Power and learn how to draw on that power to improve my life. The Steps helped me get my mind out of the way. I became open to the reality of a relationship with the God of my understanding.

My conscious contact has been growing at each Step while I was doing the work and focusing elsewhere. Step Eleven makes the development of that conscious contact specific and purposeful. Step Eleven tells me what to do and how to do it.

What are we seeking to improve?

When I started seriously into my program, the idea of a "conscious contact" with a Higher Power was very foreign to me. Still, I found the idea intriguing so, when I heard that we could take Step Eleven out of order, I dug into the idea enthusiastically. Of course, not everybody feels the need to start on Step Eleven early, but I did.

In Step Ten, we adopt the discipline of regularly examining our decisions and actions to avoid or correct "wrongs." We understand that sometimes actually figuring out right from wrong isn't obvious. Even when we know, it isn't always clear what to do after admitting a wrong. Or how to avoid it in the future. This is where Step Eleven comes in.

Remember from the discussion on Step Three how angry I got about the neighbor who blocked my view with his cargo van? I spent months being a little crazy. From my perspective today, after years in Al-Anon, I recognize this obsession with my neighbor's ugly truck as a severe lapse in the sanity I would like to have. When I think about this old insanity, I recall the Spider Robinson quote, "If a person who indulges in gluttony is a glutton, and a person who commits a felony is a felon, then God is an iron." For me and ugly trucks, God remains an iron.

It seems that where I live now, thirty years later, another neighbor parks his battered pick-up truck directly in front of the best view from my house. It's been that way for more than ten years, and I don't expect him to change his habit now. Whenever I think about it, I get a flash of annoyance and fantasize about getting even. I understand that I am powerless over his parking, but ugly thoughts about shooting tires full of holes and driving nails come to mind. I wish I could accept the situation more gracefully, so I have prayed about it.

In my prayers, I ask for tolerance, patience, and calm acceptance. From time to time, I joke with my Higher Power in my prayers, "Can't you think up a better symbol than a broken-down old truck? This isn't even interesting. Come on, challenge me with something new; I already did the truck thing."

Some people might think that prayers like this, a tease or a complaint, are disrespectful or even blasphemous. In my opinion, the better my conscious contact with the God of my understanding, the easier it is to sort out these problematic, obscure, and confusing details of real life. I think an informal tone, like the one I strike with my friends, is just right. This kind of conscious contact feels more like love.

Why does Step Eleven say I should "[seek] to improve" instead of just saying improve? The other Steps are a lot more definite — admitted, made a decision, made an inventory, asked, made a list, made amends, continued to take inventory—no equivocation in those Steps. Perhaps there are two reasons why Step Eleven is less directive.

Let's start by agreeing we are animals. We have drives and behaviors in common with other animals. We are driven to protect ourselves, slake thirst, satisfy hunger, reproduce and protect our young, and avoid pain, discomfort, and irritation. That's our animal nature. In humans, the drives are enforced within us by basic feelings: fear, anger, disgust, love, and lust. Feelings are all part of the evolutionary machinery of being a human animal.[23] Though we are animals, that is not all we are. We also have minds. Marvelous things, minds.

My mind makes it possible for me to remember, analyze, anticipate, conjecture, evaluate, compare, contrast, associate, and a multitude of other things (including writing this book). One of the remarkable things about my mind is that it convinces me that you have a mind too, and your mind makes possible all the same multitude of things (including reading this book).

The human mind is a unique gift. Human beings didn't get to be Earth's most successful species because we have a brain. We dominate the world because every man and woman has a mind. A mind is a complex and subtle factory for making choices. Experiences are the raw materials, and decisions are the products. We use the mind's tools to

---

23 I use the word "feelings" here because the term I wanted to use, basic emotions, is rife with academic turmoil. Opinions vary as to what the basic emotions are and how many there are. Many psychologists settle on six basic emotions: happiness, sadness, fear, anger, surprise, and disgust. Other psychologists prefer only four, combining fear and surprise and anger and disgust. Still, others go off in different directions entirely. I chose the term feelings to convey the internal states that I experience powerfully enough that my behavior becomes very strongly directed.

take our experience, shape it, polish it, and package it. Out comes a stream of thoughts, choices, and acts; that's what we call free will.

Opinion divides those who believe in free will from those who prefer a reductionist explanation of the complexities of human behavior. I joined the free will camp (at least metaphorically) simply because I decided to turn it (my free will) over to a Higher Power in Step Three.

In Step Eleven, I endorse the free will concept even further by asking for knowledge of God's will for me, implying that there is a distinction between my (free) will and God's will for me. The natural questions arise: how can I make my will and God's will coincide, and how will I know when I am successful?

Step Eleven suggests that I seek a conscious contact with my Higher Power and pray for knowledge of God's will, but there is precious little guidance on how to do it. The Steps leave the details up to each of us. What is comfortable for me may not fit you at all, but we all seek an answer.

The answer that comforts me is simple, and I like to express it in a "what if" story.

What if, when the universe took its first shape, and the light of the spirit was first revealed, God said, "Here are the many needed dimensions." He created up and down, here and there, now and then, inside and out, above and below, before and beyond. He declared all these and more and said, "Humans will find names for all these dimensions when names are needed." And, because there was to be free will in this universe, God said, "So that the people know my will. There will be one more dimension, a spiritual dimension, in which every choice will experience a strength and direction toward goodness or away."

It pleases me to imagine this force field of goodness in the universe and to believe that it is positive in the direction of God's will. Perhaps you have felt it; I have. I think most of us do. We somehow know the direction of goodness and health even if we sometimes turn away from it. Some call it "conscience." Some refer to an internal "still small voice." I call it the Field of Grace, and I sometimes feel it in odd ways.

For example, one day, I saw my neighbor struggling to get a large table into the back of his pick-up truck (yeah, that same old truck I hate in front of my windows). I was tempted to watch and enjoy his troubles, but I knew there was a better thing to do. I went out and helped him load the truck; then, I rode with him and helped him unload it. This was a small thing, but I could feel the direction of the Field of Grace, and I wanted to move that way.

Popular culture recognizes this feeling. We imagine the tiny devil on one shoulder and the tiny angel on the other, pointing in the positive and negative directions of the Field of Grace. I like to imagine that, as free agents, we each are equipped with a built-in sensor that can orient us in that field as birds orient themselves in the magnetic field of Earth.

Of course, my field detector is a human instrument, and the Field of Grace is a very subtle force. Evolution gave us senses to survive as a species, and they operate primarily in the physical dimensions of reality. Sadly, when I attend to the signals and drives of my animal nature, my Field of Grace detector is easily drowned out.

In the belief system I prefer, the biggest obstacle to my knowledge of God's will is my busy mind. Hence, I need to seek a conscious contact with my Higher Power through techniques — prayer and meditation — that help me set aside the busyness. Because I have a beautiful, wonderful, exquisitely complex human mind, it is not an easy matter to set it aside even temporarily and tune in to God's will. That's the first reason that Step Eleven gives me a little slack about following the directions.

I think the second reason Step Eleven suggests we "seek" to improve our conscious contact instead of using a more pedestrian verb like "work" or "struggle" is to emphasize the fact that finding the way to do it is likely to require exploration or invention. Cranking up my conscious contact with the Great Mystery isn't an everyday, pedestrian thing to do. Prayer and meditation are not activities that are built in to our human bag of tricks; we have to learn them.

Before we get into a discussion of prayer and meditation in detail, let's look more closely at the experience we call conscious contact with our Higher Power.

About conscious contact

First of all, I will assert that making conscious contact with a Higher Power is possible for anybody. I suspect that it happens to everybody from time to time. When the contact comes without preparation, it's going to be a surprise. Since it doesn't happen all that often, conscious contact is very noticeable and memorable. I recall having experiences like that before I was even remotely willing to recognize the existence of such a thing as my Higher Power.

Occasionally I would experience an overwhelming rush of emotion that would run through my whole being, last for a moment, and then gradually disappear. These feelings were indescribably good, the most pleasure I could imagine.

In memory, these experiences seem associated with positive events or perceptions — holding a sleeping newborn, the awareness of being loved, the completion of a momentous task, a recognition of some true act of goodness, witnessing heroism, or finding some important secure place. I call these experiences "spontaneous contacts" with my Higher Power.

I could never have explained the feelings, but I certainly recall them. I cherished those experiences and wanted more. Or at least I would have desired more if I had given it any thought. As it was, these beautiful experiences just happened in the course of a busy life and, if I thought about it at all, I would have said that these "happy moments" were nothing special.

On the other hand, Step Eleven tells us to seek out these experiences "to improve our conscious contact." So, the Step suggests specific actions. I want more of this conscious contact and, to get it, meditation is the preparation, and prayer is the execution.

How we do the improving

Meditation is the name I give to all the mental and physical conditioning exercises I do to put myself in shape for effective prayer. Like most worthwhile activities, Prayer requires skill to succeed, and the skill requires practice to develop. If I want to be good at prayer, I have to build some skill through practice. There is also the matter of conditioning.

I have to be in shape to play football, so I condition my body to exertion and rough contact. In contrast, prayer requires conditioning the mind to peace, openness, and focus, but it's still conditioning. Meditation is what I call this kind of conditioning. Just as good physical shape and toughness are generally worthwhile things to develop (even if I don't play football), the capabilities of mind that meditation develops are generally worthwhile in themselves and prepare me for more effective prayer.

It's fair to ask at this point, what do I mean by "effective prayer?" To answer, here's how I look at prayer in general.

Spontaneous prayers

How we pray isn't very important to working the Steps. Knees, no knees. Gestures, no gestures, Hat, no hat. Rug, no rug. Memorized or spontaneous. Formal, informal. Church, no church. And so forth. Pray the way that works for you.

Notice that three kinds of prayers seem to happen spontaneously without any conscious effort — **Help! Wow!** and **Thanks!** I don't think about it; these spontaneous prayers just happen. They burst out in response to an extraordinary experience or perception.

Everybody has these moments, and they happen entirely outside of the concepts of religion. So here's how I interpret these spontaneous prayers now that I understand to whom they are directed.

- Help! recognizes the truth that my Higher Power can change me in ways that I can't do by myself. I say it with an in-breath and a little moan.

- Wow! acknowledges the awesome nature of my Higher Power and helps me find humility. I breathe out and smile.
- Thanks! is an unconscious recognition of the existence of my Higher Power, the privilege of being a human being, and the outright gift of my Higher Power's love and care. It starts with a deep in-breath, and the word comes on a strong out-breath.

Those are spontaneous prayers and represent some of the best evidence for the spiritual dimension of reality. Spontaneous prayers are not under my rational control. They emerge from a subconscious level, my mind's basement, deep in my animal nature.

These three are "subconscious contact" with my Higher Power. But, of course, there are many other kinds of prayers and more than a little disagreement about definitions and taxonomy.

Prayers and the Twelve Steps

There are many prayers associated with the Twelve Steps. Several are drawn from the A.A. Big Book, others are based on the experiences and advice offered there.[24] Despite the avowed intention to be spiritual rather than religious, Twelve Step programs draw from the rich Christian literature of prayer, in, especially in the United States. Twelve Step meetings are likely to use the familiar Lord's Prayer[25] and the so-called St. Francis Peace Prayer cited by Bill W. in the A.A. Twelve and Twelve.[26] The prominence of these prayers in Twelve Step programs is almost certainly a consequence of the history of A.A. Neither prayer is strictly a part of a Twelve Step program unless I want it to be.

---

[24] One source of the many prayers associated with the Steps can be found on the website A.A. Big Book, Friends of Bill W., "Friends of Bill W. - Twelve Step Prayers," http://friendsofbillw.net/twelve_step_prayers (accessed February 14, 2017).

[25] Taken from Matthew 6:9–13 (ESV). When I was a newcomer to the program, I was very uncomfortable when the meeting joined hands and prayed the Lord's Prayer. So I did a special Fourth Step on my feelings and then wrote a commentary on the prayer that expressed how I could participate with the group even though I am not a Christian. I have included that interpretation in Appendix B.

[26] From *Twelve Steps and Twelve Traditions* p.99 (included in Appendix C).

The knowledge and power prayer

The particular prayer suggested in Step Eleven is what we might call the "knowledge and power" prayer. This is one example of a kind of prayer sometimes called petition or supplication, simply asking God for what we need.

Step Eleven suggests that I employ the knowledge and power prayer to improve my conscious contact with God, that is, ask for the knowledge of His will and power to carry it out. The Steps don't have anything to say about prayer for any other kind of need. Indeed, the Steps haven't anything to say about any other kind of prayer at all. We are free to understand the nature of prayer, its protocols, uses, and purposes, anyway we like.

Unlike spontaneous prayers, the knowledge and power prayer originates under my volition in my conscious mind. I intentionally use it to seek to improve my conscious contact.

It seems obvious enough that the Higher Power side of the contact is the same as in the spontaneous prayers so I have to conclude that the objective when I use the knowledge and power prayer is to somehow change me.[27] Logically then, when I pray the knowledge and power prayer, I may change in some way and my conscious contact with my Higher Power may be improved, but the result isn't certain. Is there anything I can do to improve the odds and make my "seeking" more effective? Yes, I think so.

Meditation

Let's agree that a human mind, extraordinary as it is, gets in the way of my conscious contact with my Higher Power. Certainly, then, one of the things I need to do is find ways to move my mind's busyness aside while I pray.

Meditation is the conditioning work I do so that when I pray, I can free myself from the mind's distractions and allow my consciousness to settle into contact with my Higher Power. Some say prayer is talking to God, and meditation is listening to him. That's useful as far as it goes, but I think that "listening" is too superficial a description of

---

27 In my personal view, that is what all volitional prayers do, but others may have different opinions on this point.

what I need to do to allow the God of my understanding to reach me, teach me, and change me. I prefer to think meditation is what I do to prepare myself to grow my conscious contact. Meditation is work.

The literature of meditation is truly vast. Meditation in one form or another has been part of human seeking for all of recorded history and probably precedes even that. Asian religions and philosophies have the most extended history of investigating meditation, but there is meditation in nearly every realm in which human beings examine their minds' workings.[28]

For me, meditation is any activity focused internally that gets me into this exact moment and keeps me there. Sitting works for a lot of people. Guidance can help. Walking, even running, can work. Minds don't naturally meditate; they need to practice.

The benefit of meditation is knowledge of my mind and some measure of control. Remember, I am trying to improve my conscious contact with the God of my understanding. When I observe the workings of my mind, I become better informed about the nature of the task. When I see the task more clearly, I have a better shot at controlling the parts of my mind that are getting in the way. So I practice.

The Twelve Steps don't tell me how to meditate; Step 11 asks me to use meditation as part of my seeking. I've tried various techniques and found them informative and useful to varying degrees. I suspect that we differ enough as human beings that no single plan is optimal for us all.

For me, mindfulness meditation with a focus on breathing was educational. Focusing on loving-kindness (*metta meditation*) has softened something in me that life had made very hard. I've had mixed results with various moving meditations: Yoga hasn't done much for me, but *Tai Chi* and *Qigong* directly affect how I perceive and experience my body. Your results may vary.

---

28 Here is one rundown of meditation types from website GLOOM, "Types Of Meditation: Extensive List of Techniques," Mental Health Daily, http://mentalhealthdaily.com/2015/03/24/types-of-meditation-extensive-list-of-techniques/ (accessed February 14, 2017).

What Conscious Contact feels like

Before we conclude this investigation of Step Eleven, I'd like to talk about what "conscious contact," the Step Eleven objective, feels like.

My human mind and body are designed to keep me alive in a jungle or savanna, but they prevent me, most of the time, from experiencing the divine. I think there is a little spark of divinity, a portion of spiritual light, a part of God, inside us. Most of the time, just being human dominates my perceptions, and the spiritual light is hidden. Sometimes, though — once in a while — I get to feel it.

I'm talking about real sensations. For me, the feeling seems centered in my chest but spills out around my whole body and into the surrounding space. It's an ache with a sense of softness in the center. It's a painful feeling that feels unbearably good. For me, this is joy.

The feeling seems to spring unexpectedly from empathy for a terrible loss or a breathtaking blessing. I have even felt it in response to hearing about a profound act of courage. I don't initiate these experiences; I don't know how. But I have observed that they are more likely to occur when I am in transition — maybe softened up is a better term, maybe beaten up is even better — because of my spiritual work.

Summarizing Step Eleven

Like Step Ten, I do Step Eleven every day, *Sought through prayer and meditation to improve our conscious contact with God as we understood Him, praying only for knowledge of His will for us and the power to carry that out.* Here's what I've learned about the Step.

- Ever since my Third Step decision, I've been building a relationship with the God of my understanding. Prayer and meditation are the ways I do it.
- The conscious contact is real, not a metaphor.
- Prayer and meditation don't automatically give me joy, but they make it possible for me to experience it more often. For me, joy is the conscious contact that I seek in Step Eleven. From inside, out.

It's the three As again. Step Ten is an Awareness tool; Step Eleven's prayer and meditation are the Acceptance tools. And then comes Step Twelve.

Step Twelve

Having had a spiritual awakening as the result of these steps, we tried to carry this message to others, and to practice these principles in all our affairs.

Step Twelve is about Action. The result of the Twelve Step program is a spiritual awakening. The message is, "Something wonderful has happened to me, and now I want to share it."

When I came to Al-Anon, I certainly didn't expect to have a spiritual awakening and, if asked, I would have firmly rejected the notion. Things like that just didn't happen to people like me. So, okay, I was wrong.

I have had a spiritual awakening, and it would seem natural at this point in this book for me to tell you what it's like and how to know when it happens

Spiritual awakening

Many people — in the U.S. more than half — have an experience that they would comfortably call a spiritual awakening. Many people, certainly nearly everyone who has worked a Twelve Step program, knows the feeling. Still, it's hard to describe a spiritual awakening without venturing into flights of poetry or metaphor. Something is certainly going on; the poetry's power lies in the underlying commonality of this experience. But what exactly is going on?

Different people describe it in different ways. So perhaps the experience of spiritual awakening is unique from one person to the next. However, change is the common ingredient.

Things change. Before a spiritual awakening, I was one person, and now I am different. Of course, that's not magic. I'm a different person today than I was yesterday and different yesterday from the day before, etc., etc. It's not just that I am different that makes it a spiritual awakening. The changes have a particular set of qualities that are identifiable but difficult to pin down.

I researched spiritual awakening to try to get a handle on it, and I came up with descriptions that will give you an idea of the general qualities we're talking about.[29] The following are summaries of various sources who are describing a spiritual awakening. Read them for flavor.

- *Thinking will change.* You will be more sharply tuned into your own thinking — awareness of negative habits, clarity about reality, more intuition, increased inspiration, and creativity. You will lose interest in worrying, conflict, judgment of others, or anything superficial or inauthentic.
- *Desires will change.* You will want greater personal freedom, more meaning in your life, more connection with nature, and more spiritual connection. You will want less "stuff."
- *Feelings and emotions will change.* You will feel things more deeply. You will have waves of emotion from deep sadness to great compassion to moments of joy and bliss. You will have a sense of oneness and harmony with nature and your fellow humans. There will be new experiences. You will experience increased "coincidences" and "synchronicities" in your life. You will have episodes of intense energy, power surges, and bursts of creativity. Teachers will appear.
- *There may be bodily changes.* Hypersensitivity and amplification of the senses. Changes in sleep patterns. Changes in eating habits and food sensitivities.

I personally have experienced many of these changes, but I don't think any particular set of changes can be definitely labeled a "spiritual awakening." As human beings, we are

---

[29] The research was by no means scholarship. I took the text of the first half-dozen Google entries under "spiritual awakening" and boiled them down. The entries all described the signs of a spiritual awakening. They had various numbers of signs: 9 signs, 21 signs, etc. One had 51 signs. Some of the "signs" were quite peculiar, so I focused on the commonalities. There was a surprising amount of consistency for such a nebulous topic.

too diverse and complex, and spirituality is too subtle for a single well-defined "official" spiritual awakening experience. We change in different ways, and we experience those changes through a lens of personal experience. On the other hand, there is clearly something that happens and enough commonality of experience to recognize spiritual awakening as a real phenomenon. The changes described as a spiritual awakening are deeply resonant with the A.A. and Al-Anon promises summarized on page 1 at the beginning of the book.

It's worthwhile to ask, "what's going on" with this spiritual awakening thing? All the answers I am aware of are either mythological, religious, or reductionist (science boiling these changes down to the chemical consequences of experience). As usual, the Steps don't give us any guidance on this topic. Instead, we get to understand the nature of the phenomenon as we wish. Here's my way.

My choice is fanciful but comforting to me.

- I choose to believe that the spiritual dimension of the universe is as real as the physical dimensions.
- As creatures who have evolved in this complex reality, we can sense and experience the spiritual dimension. It's a built-in part, another sense.
- I believe that, just as the mind is an emergent property of life (agency), perception of the spiritual universe is an emergent property of mind. Human minds have a potentially sensitive ability built into our brain parts.
- In my opinion, the work I do while pursuing a spiritual path conditions my physical body — especially the brain parts — and frees me of the (otherwise over-whelming) stream of consciousness to use the emergent spiritual perception ability.

So, I explain what's going on like this. I did the Steps, which are a series of spiritual exercises. The exercises and experiences that I have while working my program change my brain to strengthen my ability to perceive the spiritual dimension of reality. The sensations of encountering the spiritual dimension are new to me and strange, so I think, feel, and act differently than I did before. I have had a spiritual awakening, I am changed, and my life is different.

Step Twelve says that as a result of doing the Steps, I have had a spiritual awakening and suggests that having had one, I carry the message. So that's the next thing for us to think about.

Carrying the message

Bill W. wrote a whole chapter in the A.A. Big Book about Step Twelve (Chapter 7 *Working with others* p.89) and another substantial explanation of the Twelfth Step in the A.A. Twelve and Twelve.[30] His perspective was: now that we have got our miracle, we need to share it with the others who are still suffering the way we suffered. He was precise about the kind of suffering he was referring to — alcoholism. He acknowledged the disruption that the disease raises in families, but his focus was clearly on carrying the message to alcoholics.

The wives of A.A. members were the founders of Al-Anon. They applied the A.A. spiritual program to their own lives. Quickly Al-Anon grew to be a program not just for wives but for all family and friends of alcoholics. As part of this change in emphasis, Step Twelve was modestly amended in Al-Anon's Twelfth Step to suggest carrying the message "to others" rather than to the narrower version in the A.A. Twelfth Step, which says "to alcoholics." In my opinion, this modest change makes an enormous conceptual difference.

In the A.A. Big Book, Bill W. writes about seeking out other alcoholics to share experience and, if it's welcome, to encourage them to follow the program outlined in the Steps. When Bill wrote the Twelve and Twelve, he broadened the approach to emphasize the value of sharing experience in A.A. meetings. Still, A.A.'s Twelfth Step focus is specifically aiding suffering alcoholics. Al-Anon is different.

The "others" to whom Al-Anon seeks to carry the message are specifically the friends and families of alcoholics. I've often wondered why, if so many friends and family

---

[30] *Twelve Steps and Twelve Traditions* pp. 106-125.

members are affected by a single alcoholic, there aren't a lot more people in Al-Anon than in A.A. At the very least, Al-Anon Twelfth Step work has a much larger potential audience.

I imagine the answer at the heart of this question is Awareness. As the disease of alcoholism progresses, it becomes more and more difficult to ignore or deny that there is a drinking problem. Eventually, denial becomes impossible for anyone paying attention (except, perhaps, the drinker). The need for a solution to the drinker's problem becomes painfully clear. On the other hand, as a codependent, it is so much more difficult for me to realize that I have a problem. Most people who come to Al-Anon are there at first to solve someone else's problem. Only if I stay long enough do I come to see that the focus for recovery must shift to me. That's why the most important thing we say to newcomers is "keep coming back."

As a codependent, the root of my problem is a misunderstanding about responsibility and a lack of clarity about what I can control and what I can't. Therefore, the Serenity Prayer and "the wisdom to know the difference" is the pivot on which my recovery depends.

The Stoic philosophers built a whole way of living around solving this problem. They believed that clarity about the extent of each person's control was a key to a successful life and that, in truth, the only thing we can control is our mind.

In our Twelve Step programs, we talk about a "disease" of mind, body, and spirit. In my opinion, this "disease" is, in fact, the same underlying condition for alcoholics, addicts, or compulsives of various kinds, those affected by these behaviors, and anyone else who, for whatever reason, fails to grasp the limits of personal control and operates with a clouded mind. The disease expresses itself differently in different people because of our diversity of biology, genetics, and experience. Therefore, I believe a Twelve Step program applies to an enormous range of human problems and experiences.

For me, the others to whom I seek to carry the message are all those with any condition of mind — addiction, delusion, or denial — that provokes suffering.

Service

Carrying the message is referred to as a vital purpose of Al-Anon, and Al-Anon calls the actions of carrying the message "service." The scope of Al-Anon service is summed up this way:

> *"Anything done to help a relative or friend of an alcoholic is service: a telephone call to a despairing member or sponsoring a newcomer, telling one's story at meetings, forming groups, arranging for public information, distributing literature, and financially supporting groups, local services, and the World Service Office."*[31]

Al-Anon has codified their understanding of service in a set of twelve Concepts of Service and five General Warranties which provide the foundation for the functioning of Al-Anon as an organization. It's beyond the scope of this book to get into the philosophical and operational details, but I mention it here to point out that "carrying the message" can be either a very personal thing or it can mean participating in the organization at any level from local group to worldwide. This is another "take what you want and leave the rest" subject.

My experience of service started with arranging chairs and laying out the literature at meetings. After six months, my sponsor suggested I could chair a meeting which I did with great seriousness and more than a little trepidation. I didn't want to get it wrong. Eventually I noticed that the mood of the meeting depended a lot less on the preparation or the skill of the leader than on the mysterious spiritual dynamics of a group. So I relaxed.

My sponsor gradually encouraged me to take on a variety of roles in my Al-Anon home group, then pushed me gently

---

[31] *Al-Anon Alateen Service Manual*, Introduction to Concepts.

into positions at the district level. Before that I had never given any thought to there actually being any organization to Al-Anon. I was much too focused on my own situation to wonder how all of the organizational things got done.

After a couple of years I was even involved with Al-Anon's regional activities. Along with these organizational-type service activities I did a similar progression of personal service, mostly sponsorship and speaking. These experiences were essential to my recovery as I gave up my isolation and began to see my defects of character play out in yet another context. Lots of "aha" moments.

It's about twenty years now since my first Al-Anon meeting and my first encounter with the Twelve Steps and my first tentative ventures into service work. I endorse 100% A.A.'s focus on carrying the message to alcoholics and Al-Anon's focus on carrying the message to families and friends of alcoholics, but I have gradually become convinced that the idea of service is even wider.

When the topic is carrying the message we often hear that a Twelve Step program is for "someone who wants it, not someone who needs it." We can't force a Twelve Step program on someone and it's foolish to try. We can, however, be an example of the benefits of the program to everyone we meet and, regardless of their situation (addiction, compulsion, collateral damage, or lost serenity) we can model and, when asked, can explain what we have been through, what we've done, and how it's worked for us. No more is required. No more is desired.

Traditionally Twelve Step members have carried the message, primarily in our meeting rooms, by personal contact and support. In addition, we pray in the Third Step Prayer that our lives can bear witness "to those [we] would help." In A.A. one can often hear "I may be the only example of the Big Book that some people ever see."

The idea that my recovery and the changes I have experienced can, by example, be the message I seek to carry seems powerful to me and I can think of no reason whatsoever why the positive influence of carrying the message shouldn't be focused outward beyond some target group to all creatures. Carrying the message is the logical bridge to the last part of Step Twelve, "practice these principles in all our affairs."

Principles

When we come to the last phrase in Step Twelve, we are once again confronted with ambiguity. What are the principles we try to practice?

Let's turn to the dictionary for help. We find "principle" defined as "a fundamental truth or proposition that serves as the foundation for a system of belief or behavior or for a chain of reasoning." Unfortunately, in Twelve Step literature and lore, the word principle is rarely used as either a "truth" or a "proposition." Instead, the word is almost universally used to denote a virtue.[32] Furthermore, writers of Twelve Step literature generally don't agree about which virtues we ought to try to practice in all our affairs.

Because of this confusion, I did another little research project similar to the one on spiritual awakening. In a half-dozen high profile enumerations of these "principles" I found the names of 38 virtues or virtuous states of mind. The sixteen of these mentioned in two or more of the sources were:

Humility	14	Faith	3
Willingness	10	Generosity	3
Acceptance	7	Courage	2
Forgiveness	6	Gratitude	2
Honesty	6	Patience	2
Open-mindedness	5	Strength	2
Tolerance	5	Understanding	2
Love	4	Wisdom	2

It's possible to quibble over definitions or conceptual subtleties. Personally, I would rearrange the order, but this is a pretty good list as a guide to behavior. Like nearly

---

[32] According to the same dictionary, virtue is "behavior showing high moral standards."

everything else in a Twelve Step program, however, I get to make my own list of the virtues I believe constitute a good life. Then I seek to practice whatever principles I adhere to that produce such a life.

Just for fun, here are the other virtues that were mentioned in the sources I analyzed.

Calmness	Fortitude	Persistence
Compassion	Good-Judgment	Prudence
Discipline	Harmony	Selflessness
Fairness	Kindness	Self-restraint
Fearlessness	Objectivity	Service
Forthrightness	Optimism	Sincerity
Thoroughness	Truthfulness	Unselfishness

This is a pretty good list too. Life is complex, and we have an enormous number of ways to exhibit the positive results of Twelve Step recovery. But, again, part of the power of the Steps is the tremendous flexibility I have in understanding it and practicing it.

Summarizing Step Twelve

This Step says, "Having had a spiritual awakening as the result of these steps, we tried to carry this message to others, and to practice these principles in all our affairs." But it might as well say, "Keep going, spread the word, have a good life."

Steps Ten and Eleven are the Awareness and Acceptance components of my continuing spiritual growth. Step Twelve is all about the third A, Action.

Sanity, my original health, is realized as wisdom, compassion, and loving-kindness; these conditions arise in my spirit and inhabit my mind. But without action, that's where they stay, goodness teetering on the edge of being. So I make them real through my actions.

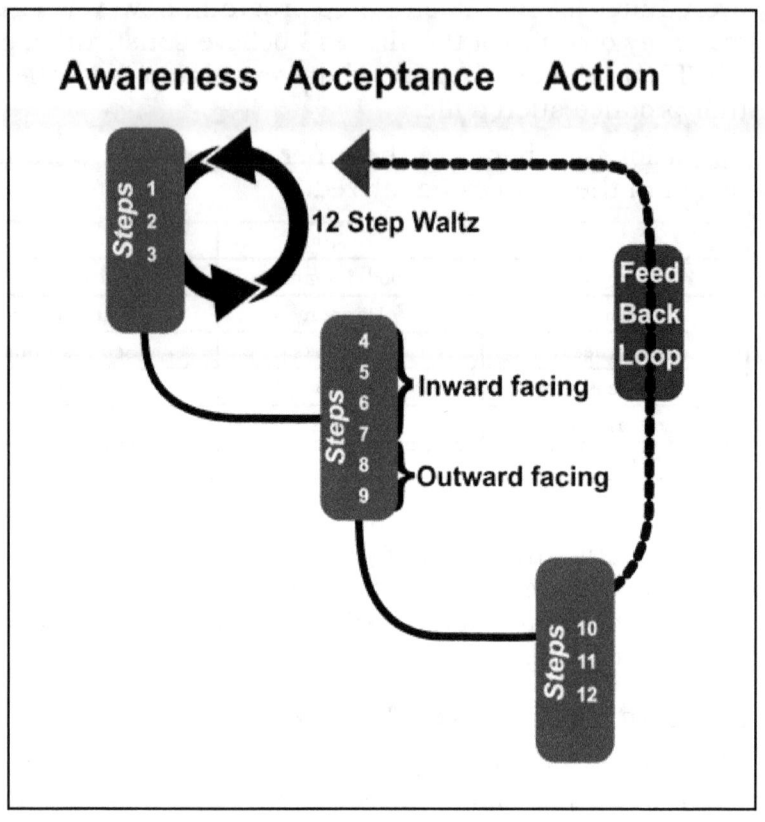

What Now?

THIS BOOK HAS BEEN ABOUT THE STEPS as I experienced them in Al-Anon. However, I don't want to leave the impression that I have covered all of the excellent dimensions of the Al-Anon program. Al-Anon is not a self-help program. An Al-Anon family group is a community and has comfort, healing, and wisdom to offer beyond the Steps. Furthermore, there are important topics in Al-Anon that don't emerge from the Steps alone. For instance:

- Boundaries
- Detachment
- Forgiveness
- Self-care
- Communication and Conflict resolution

Since you've read this far, you no doubt have a pretty good idea of how this one recovering Al-Anon member views the Twelve Steps. I've said that excellent as the Steps are, they are not the whole of a spiritual path, and just having done the Steps does not entirely assure us the good life we want. We may find our spiritual path and community through Al-Anon or A.A. or another Twelve Step program, but the path continues beyond the Steps.

The Steps make a good life possible, but we have to live it. So what is living that life like?

Back in the discussion of Step Ten, I gave my opinion of what maturity means, and I said, "Growing into maturity is the process of living a good life." What follows is a description of how I think this looks in everyday life. But, again, to be clear, the report I give here shows my choices, inclinations, and preferences. Yours may vary.

Understanding

Since maturity comes from understanding, expending time and energy trying to understand things is part of the good life. Unfortunately, I can't understand everything, so I need to focus.

- First, I try to focus on understanding myself: what I do, how well my actions match the person I'd like to be, and how I might get better at being that person.
- Second, I try to understand the immense forces that drive how the human species evolves. Some of this is about biology and biochemistry, but mostly it's about understanding history, primarily how technology and human nature interact.
- Third, I try to understand how human beliefs, values, principles, and mental models are expressed in our social groups' norms and actions, especially our laws, regulations, and social etiquette.

Getting clarity about the nature of reality and maintaining a firm grasp of the obvious seems to be a necessary prerequisite to understanding. Still, perfect clarity is illusory, and reality is very slippery.

Discernment

Since maturity requires discernment, I seek to distinguish real from unreal, healthy from unhealthy, and wise from unwise. I strive to control myself, but many things are outside my control. Nevertheless, I am part of a complex society, and I have a role to play. I influence, in large and small ways, how reality evolves in the world. I may not be correct in my opinions and intentions, but I have a responsibility to be able to explain why they are what they are.

I try to resist the impulse to throw up my hands and say, "Whatever!"

Character

Understanding and discernment are important and valuable qualities to cultivate, but they are intellectual and feel chilly. So I also seek to develop my character to be as full of the warmth and sap of life as I can be.

I wish for my character to combine compassion and wisdom with strength and courage. I wish my sympathy and empathy to be genuine, not merely conventional. I struggle against indifference, and I reproach myself when I am aware of moral cowardice or willful ignorance. But, then, before I treat myself too severely, I find a little compassion for myself and usually a little amusement too at how "human" it is to be a human being.

Responsibility

My Twelve Step program encouraged me to understand clearly the things I cannot control. However, I must take responsibility for the things I can control. My beliefs, values, and principles are mine even though they may have formed more-or-less unnoticed in my childhood and during the stresses and chaos of loving an addicted person. I have a responsibility to examine these roots of my mind, own them, and change them if necessary.

Furthermore, I am responsible for my actions. "The devil made me do it, I couldn't help myself, and it's all her fault," simply won't wash. If I did it, it's mine. Likewise, if my actions are worthy, I should own them too. Modesty may be a virtue, but false modesty is a kind of arrogance. So instead, I would like to seek humility.

Moderation and balance

Ralph Waldo Emerson usually gets credit for saying "Moderation in all things," but the idea has been around for a long time. Pretty much as long as people have been thinking about how to have a good life. My Twelve Step program didn't have anything specific to say about moderation, but I could see right away that going to extremes was a losing strategy.

I've come to believe that a good life is lived down the center of the metaphorical road. I don't see life dominated by overly strict "strait gates" and a "narrow way," but I'm pretty clear that radicalism and absolutism are not what I want either. So I try to avoid overreaction, extremism, and fundamentalism of any kind. I try to avoid serious self-indulgence, and I try to keep abstinence private.

Reverence and tolerance

An unavoidable consequence of being human seems to be that faith and doubt are inseparable. My recovery through the Steps introduced me to a life involving faith in a Higher Power that cares for me. My human conditioning, rationality, and skeptical nature introduced me to a constant back and forth between faith and doubt. I understand and accept the struggle.

One consequence of my struggle is a more profound respect for the struggles others have had and still have with faith and doubt. I am willing to accept and respect the various beliefs, tools, and faith rituals they use in their struggles and treat them with reverence. Tolerance extends to those who have lost the struggle and advocate atheism and agnosticism. Even to those who ridicule faith. I see their human struggle as the same as mine.

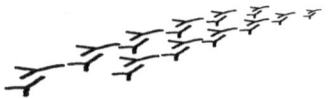

This brings us to the end of this little book. Thank you for staying with me this far. The chance to write and explain what I have experienced and learned in my Twelve Step recovery has been a privilege for which I am grateful. I hope the message that I have carried will contribute to your understanding and that you, too, will come to live the better life the Steps have promised us.

Appendixes

Appendix A
Step Four Guide[33]

This approach to Step Four "Made a searching and fearless moral inventory of ourselves" is structured into five parts. Take three or four days for each part. The actual time will vary greatly depending on how hard you work and how deep you go, but assume that you can finish the Step in less than a month.

Make an appointment for your Fifth Step no more than a month from right now. Plan to keep it.

Fourth Step Suggestions Part 1

About Part 1

The Fourth Step cannot be complete unless it is fearless and searching.

You cannot afford to look away from things you wish not to see. Only you will know when you have searched thoroughly. Only you will know if you have faced the things that you fear. This Step will change your life for the better in direct proportion to your willingness to face the fear and do the work.

If you haven't read the Fourth Step sections in the Big Book, How Al-Anon Works, the Twelve and Twelve, and Paths to Recovery, do it before you start this work.

The Work for Part 1

Begin the Big Book format for analyzing your resentments. [Four column worksheet or equivalent]

I resent	What happened or what I resent	What was threatened	

Start with a list of every person, place, institution, policy, principle, or idea that you resent [Column 1.].

Just make the list. Think over your life thoroughly, especially your youth. Don't be surprised if you find people you love or even God on this list. This may be a long list.

When the list is done, write a brief statement explaining what happened, what you

---

[33] I created this approach to Step Four for some of the men I sponsored. The material is not copyrighted so feel free to use it or any of its parts.

resent [Column 2], and what part of your life was threatened that produced this resentment — self-esteem security, personal relations, sexual relations or pride [Column 3]. When you have documented the resentments, put the list aside for awhile, leaving Column 4 blank..

Congratulations! You have just started one of the most important things you've ever done. Ask your Sponsor for Part 2.

Fourth Step Suggestions Part 2

Confront your fears. Courage is not being unafraid; courage is walking through the fear. We pray for courage in the Serenity Prayer. Here is where we do our part to get it.

About Part 2

Sometimes we hear, "Fear is a failure of faith." True enough, but not all that helpful. Fear is an emotion, a quantity of energy, which arises from the body's limbic system on orders from various parts of the brain. The hard-science view is that fear is the sensation experienced when certain complex chemicals are secreted into our bloodstream and begin to interact with various organ systems. Most of us don't like this feeling and will go to extremes to avoid feeling it even though, within a few minutes, blood chemistry dissolves away all traces of the causes.

In most cases the limbic system gets kicked into action by mental events that happen below the level of consciousness. Did you ever have a scare in traffic and know that you were aware of the adrenaline rush of fright even before you figured out what happened? Most of our fear reactions are like that, arising out of old pathways in our brains that operate below the level of ordinary awareness. In this part of your Fourth Step, you will uncover some of those unconscious pathways. Examining the associations that cause us fear is useful in order to test whether or not the fears are reasonable or, perhaps, just leftovers from a previous time in our lives.

The Work for Part 2

Make a two column worksheet like this:

What I fear	Why

In the first column write down the things that you are afraid of. For example: I'm afraid I'll lose my (job, wife, parents, children's respect); I'm afraid of (open spaces, high places, closed in places, dark places). I'm afraid of (conflict, failure, success); I'm afraid of (death, old age, sickness); I'm afraid of (being poor, appearing to be poor, losing what I have); or I'm afraid that people will know that (I'm faking it, I'm ugly inside, I'm afraid).

In the second column do your best to explain why you think you are afraid of this particular thing, experience, etc. If you don't know, that's okay. If you'd like to guess, that'd be good. It might be useful in understanding why, to try to remember when this particular fear started.

After you've completed your list, write the answers to these two questions about each of your fears:

- In what way does this fear serve me?
- In what way does this fear limit my life?

If you have trouble with these two questions, ask your sponsor for some examples or specific help.

Congratulations! You will never feel quite the same way about these fears again. Ask your Sponsor for Part 3.

Fourth Step Suggestions Part 3

Rationalization is a stronger human drive than the need for sex. If you don't believe that, just think how often you go a day without a rationalization … (laugh at this point).

About Part 3

The old joke is only funny because we all understand how important a drive sex is. In this part we are asked to shine a light on this important area of our lives which so frequently is shrouded in denial, obscured by social correctness, and surrounded in shame or embarrassment.

Remember, the value of this inventory depends on how honest we are. Don't let this deteriorate into salaciousness, but don't hide important details either. Your Higher Power already knows what went on, and, believe it or not, there is nothing new under the sun. Whatever you include in your inventory, it has already been on someone else's before.

The Work for Part 3

Examine your sexual conduct. Make a three column worksheet like this:

Sexual relationship	What happened	

In the first column list every sexual relationship you have had in your life, beginning with your first explorations. Don't leave anything out — first kiss, serious fantasy objects (even if you never met), one night stands, and serious relationships. If you're straight, also include any homo-erotic experience. If you're gay, also include any hetero-erotic experience.

In the second column comment on each. Note especially if you were selfish, dishonest, or inconsiderate. Did you hurt that person? Did you hurt someone else? Did you hurt yourself? Did you unjustifiably arouse jealousy, suspicion, or bitterness? Be specific.

After you've completed your list and the comments, put the list aside for awhile, leaving column 3 blank.

Congratulations! Ask your Sponsor for Part 4.

Fourth Step Suggestions Part 4

Our Higher Power didn't create us to fail. Each of us has the strengths and assets we need for a successful life. Sometimes it takes a searching and fearless inventory to see them clearly.

About Part 4

Some of us in Al-Anon have been convinced that the chaos in our lives is our fault. Many of us have said to ourselves, "If I could only be a better (person, spouse, lover, provider, kid, housekeeper, cook, parent, etc.), the drinking/chaos/craziness would stop." We know better now, but many of the feelings of being "less than" or "not good enough" or "at fault" or "inadequate" have stuck with us. In this part we look at the reality of our assets, and shine the light of clarity on lies we believed about ourselves. We identify the strengths we can build on.

The Work for Part 4

Investigate your assets.

- **Make a list of your personal strengths** — intelligence, creativity, strength, sensitivity, and so forth. Give an example or otherwise explain how this personal strength has exhibited itself in your life. Work on this until you have found at least seven personal strengths.

- **Make a list of positive things that you bring to relationships** — honesty, dependability, kindness, gentleness, loyalty, and so forth. Give an example or otherwise explain how this positive aspect of your personality has exhibited itself in your relationships. Work on this until you have found at least seven ways that you make a positive contribution to your relationships.

- **Write an essay entitled: I am a good person because ...** Write about your personal strengths, the contributions you make to your relationships, and about how these strengths and contributions have produced good results in your life, in the lives of the people you love, or for your community. If you have trouble seeing how your assets have contributed positively in the past, write about how they can contribute in the future. Write at least a page, more is better. If this repeats things you described in the previous two sections, that's okay.

- **Thank your Higher Power for the gifts and assets of character that you have been given.** Do it in detail. If this is hard to do, do it every day for a week. If it is still hard to do, do it for another week. Repeat as required.

Congratulations! Ask your Sponsor for Part 5.

Fourth Step Suggestions Part 5

One of the important things that comes from our "searching and fearless moral inventory" is an understanding of how our own behavior has contributed to the problems in our lives. In this last part we look at our part.

About Part 5

So far in this inventory you have listed resentments, investigated fears, reviewed your sexual history, and cataloged your assets. In this part, look for patterns. As you work, think about how your fears played a part in your relationships. Think about how your assets and your fears pulled against each other. Was there something that you did again and again? What drove that behavior?

The Work for Part 5

1. For each resentment that you wrote about in Part 1, write in Column 4 what your part was in the events that brought on the resentment. This is about you. Don't make excuses or explain what someone else's part was. It is possible for a resentment to arise without any participation on your part at all, but it is very rare. If you feel you have a case like that, review it with your sponsor.

2. For each entry in your sex inventory from part 3, write down in Column 3 what your part was in any problems in the relationship. Maybe there weren't any problems; that may be unusual, but that's okay.

3. Examine all of these new entries in parts 1 and 3 carefully. Write down any patterns you see in your behavior. Compare this information with what you wrote about fears in part 2 and note any connections.

4. The Big Book says that it is useful to identify our defects of character from this classic list: pride, greed, lust, anger, gluttony, envy, and sloth (laziness). Note which of these play a part in your resentments, fears, and relationships. For any that appear frequently or seem to be particularly important, write a brief essay about how each character defect has affected you life.

5. By this time you should have a pretty clear idea of where your fears and behaviors led you to do "wrong." Keep in mind that not every relationship has a "wrong" hiding in it. In preparation for your Fifth Step, review all of the material in all five parts of this Fourth Step, and identify "wrongs." If new things come to mind, add them in the various parts where they fit, or, if they don't fit, just write them down. If you feel like it belongs in your Fourth Step, it does!

Congratulations, you have completed your Fourth Step! You've worked very hard. It's okay to be pleased with yourself. After doing all this, the Fifth Step is easy. Tell your sponsor that you're ready.

Appendix B
Commentary on The Lord's Prayer

Our Father,
This phrase invokes for me my Higher Power. It personalizes God for me, making explicit that I can have direct communication with Him.

who art in Heaven
Heaven, to me, is the natural order of the universe. It is most evident in the Field of Grace that God has given us. It is where we end up when we cease to resist aligning our will with His. This phrase acknowledges that a caring Higher Power exists in the universe.

Hallowed be thy name.
This is my signal to me that God is the Higher Power and invoking His name triggers prayer communication which, in my opinion, is a different state of being.

Thy Kingdom Come.
For me this phrase acknowledges the awesome inevitability of God. God exists whether or not I agree. By agreeing, I take down some of the barriers that I have erected separating me from Him.

Thy Will Be Done on Earth as it is in Heaven.
This is, in my opinion, a shorthand request that my free will be aligned with God's will. It acknowledges that the exercise of free will, not aligned with God's will, is a source of imperfection and pain, and it raises the hope that being sensitive to the Field of Grace (aligning with God's will) can make Earth a better place to be.

Give us this day our daily bread.
This phrase acknowledges the fundamental importance of a connection with God. If I make that connection, I have the spiritual sustenance I require. If I fail to, my soul starves.

Forgive us our trespasses
In my free will, sometimes I turn away from the Field of Grace, the direction that is best for me. Sometimes these diversions hurt others. In my opinion, this prayer acknowledges these departures from God's will and focuses me on the immediate availability of God to those who seek him.

as we forgive those who trespass against us.
I know that, just as I am not perfect in following God's will, so other people are imperfect as well. This phrase reminds me to give up blame.

And lead us not into temptation but deliver us from evil.
This is my request for sensitivity to God's will and strength to follow it. Most dreadful to me is the evil of knowing God's will and turning away from it.

For thine is the kingdom and the power and the glory for ever and ever.
This phrase sums up my gratitude for the knowledge of the unlimited presence of a caring Higher Power in my life.

Amen.
This says I am stepping back from the special mode of being that is prayer, safe in the knowledge that I am in my Higher Power's care.

Appendix C

St. Francis Peace Prayer

Lord, make me an instrument of your peace:
where there is hatred, let me sow love;
where there is injury, pardon;
where there is doubt, faith;
where there is despair, hope;
where there is darkness, light;
where there is sadness, joy.

O divine Master, grant that I may not so much seek
to be consoled as to console,
to be understood as to understand,
to be loved as to love.
For it is in giving that we receive,
it is in pardoning that we are pardoned,
and it is in dying that we are born to eternal life.
Amen.

Appendix D
Glossary of Ambiguous Twelve Step Terms

Acceptance
As used throughout a Twelve Step program, acceptance means a firm grasp of reality. It does not imply approval, agreement, or willingness.

Admitting
As used in Steps One and Ten, admit means to invite reality into my conscious and subconscious mind.

Decision
As used in Step Three, a decision is a choice among alternatives.

Defect of character
As used in Step Six, character defects are deeply-held mistaken beliefs that are false, misleading, or oversimplified. Wrong beliefs that motivate patterns of unwise behavior in our lives.

Harm
As used in Step Eight, harm is the result of an unwise action. Including unwanted consequences such as injuries, disappointments, or failures.

Humility
As used throughout Al-Anon, humility means *a proper understanding of my relationship to my Higher Power* and being "right-sized" in relationship with God and other people.

Appendix

Moral Inventory

As used in Step Four, moral inventory means examining your history, seeing the events and your feelings about the events clearly, then looking fearlessly for truth about yourself.

Sanity

As used in Step Two, sanity is a combination of mental, physical, and spiritual health.

Shortcoming

As used in Step Seven, a shortcoming is a special kind of unwise behavior — I know what to do, but I come up short — a "shortcoming."

Wrong

As used in Step Five, the unwise choices and the consequent unwanted results.

References

Alcoholics Anonymous. *Living Sober, Some methods A.A. members have used for not drinking.* New York: Alcoholics Anonymous World Services, Inc., 1998.

Alcoholics Anonymous. *Twelve Steps and Twelve Traditions.* New York: Alcoholics Anonymous World Services, Inc., 1981.

Alcoholics Anonymous. *Alcoholics Anonymous, The Story of How Many Thousands of Men and Women Have Recovered from Alcoholism (third edition).* New York: Alcoholics Anonymous World Services, Inc., 1976.

Alcoholics Anonymous. *"Pass it on" : the story of Bill Wilson and how the A.A. message reached the world.* New York: Alcoholics Anonymous World Services, 1984. Print.

Al-Anon Family Groups. *Al-Anon Alateen Service Manual 2000-2002.* New York: Al-Anon Family Group Headquarters, 2000. Print.

Al-Anon Family Groups. *Al-Anon faces alcoholism.* New York: Al-Anon Family Group Headquarters, 1984. Print.

Al-Anon Family Groups. *Al-Anon's Twelve Steps and Twelve Traditions.* Virginia Beach, Virginia: Al-Anon Family Groups Headquarters Inc., 1981.

Al-Anon Family Groups. *As we understood— : a collection of spiritual insights by Al-Anon and Alateen members.* New York, N.Y.: Al-Anon Family Group Headquarters, 1985. Print.

Al-Anon Family Groups. *BLUEPRINT FOR PROGRESS: Al-Anon's Fourth Step Inventory*, Virginia Beach, VA, Al-Anon Family Group Headquarters, Inc.,1976

Al-Anon Family Groups. *BLUEPRINT FOR PROGRESS: Al-Anon's Fourth Step Inventory REVISED*, Virginia Beach, VA, Al-Anon Family Group Headquarters, Inc., 2004

Al-Anon Family Groups. *Courage to Change, One Day at a Time in Al-Anon II.* Virginia Beach, Virginia: Al-Anon Family Groups Headquarters Inc., 1997.

References

Al-Anon Family Groups. *How Al-Anon Works for Families & Friends of Alcoholics*. Virginia Beach, Virginia: Al-Anon Family Groups Headquarters Inc., 1995.

Al-Anon Family Groups. *Having Had a Spiritual Awakening*. Virginia Beach, Virginia: Al-Anon Family Groups Headquarters Inc., 1998.

Al-Anon Family Groups. *Hope for Today*. Virginia Beach, VA, Al-Anon Family Groups, 2002. Print.

Al-Anon Family Groups. *ONE DAY AT A TIME IN AL-ANON*, Virginia Beach, VA, Al-Anon Family Group Headquarters, Inc.,1968

Al-Anon Family Groups . *Paths to Recovery*, Virginia Beach, VA, Al-Anon Family Group Headquarters, Inc.,1997

Beattie, Melody. *The Language of Letting Go*. Center City, MN.: Hazelden, 1990.

Beattie, Melody. *Codependents' Guide to the Twelve Steps*. New York: Simon & Schuster, 1990.

Hamilton. B. *Twelve step sponsorship : how it works*. Center City, Minn: Hazelden, 1996. Print.

Hasenyager, Bruce W., *Bird Feet in Concrete:366 Daily Meditations for Thoughtful Twelve Step Seekers*. Plano Texas, AshaPress, 2015.

Knapp, Caroline., *Drinking : a love story*. New York: Dial Press, 1996. Print.

Laude, Patrick, ed. *Pray Without Ceasing: The Way of the Invocation in World Religions*. Treasures of the World's Religions. Bloomington, Ind.: World Wisdom, ©2006.

Smith, Carol C. *Recovering couples : building partnership the twelve-step way*. New York: Bantam Books, 1992. Print.

Bird Feet and the Twelve Steps

Index

Index

A

AA Big Book. See Big Book
AA promises. See promises
acceptance 24, 109, 142
Action 15
Admitting 20, 59, 142
Al-Anon promises. See promises
amends 62, 82–91, 110
Awareness 15

B

Being human 99
Big Book 2, 15, 16, 21, 48, 49
Bird Feet In Concrete 2, 3, 156
Blueprint for Progress 51, 52, 53

C

Carrying the message 122–125
Character 7, 130
Clancy Fourth Step 50
conscious contact 97, 99, 107–117

D

Defects of character 70, 70–74
Discernment 7, 130

E

entirely ready 44, 62, 63, 68, 71, 74, 75, 76, 81, 85

F

feelings 1, 13, 35, 42, 48, 50, 52, 53, 58, 62, 71, 73, 83, 110, 113, 115, 137, 143
Fourth Step, Clancy I. 50
Fourth Step, original 49
Fourth Steps, Al-Anon 51

G

good life, what's it like? 105–106

H

harm 58, 59, 70, 72, 74, 82, 83, 84, 85, 87, 88, 89, 91, 142
Higher Power 30–36, 40–46, 59–67, 79–86, 98–115
How change happens 96
humility 64, 79, 115, 131, 142

I

insanity. See sanity
inventory. See moral inventory or personal inventory

K

knowledge and power prayer 116

L

Lord's Prayer, Commentary on the 139
low bottom 4, 10

M

meditation 25–27, 49, 107–118
minds 15, 21, 68, 73, 95, 99, 101, 102, 110, 117, 121
Moderation and balance 7, 131
moral inventory 46, 47, 49, 53, 55, 134, 137, 143

P

Paying attention 77, 97, 107
personal inventory 95, 107
Personal responsibility. See Responsibility
Personal stories
   What it was like 6–11
   What happened 11–13
   What it's like now 13–14
   My Step Two journey 22–27
   What should I call my Higher Power? 33–34
   My experience of service 124
powerless 16–21, 33, 41–43, 109
practice these principles 126–127
prayer and meditation 107, 113

prayers 25, 27, 97, 108, 109, 114–117
Principles 126
promises 1, 2, 13, 29, 121

R

Responsibility 7, 35, 131
Reverence and tolerance 7, 132

S

sanity 20, 28, 32, 43, 93, 104, 105, 109, 143
Serenity Prayer 19, 43, 135
Service 124, 127, 144
shortcomings 76
spiritual awakening 15, 31, 102–105, 119–122
spiritual path 15, 62, 75, 99, 99–107, 129
sponsors 38, 47, 48, 50, 51, 91
Spontaneous prayers 114, 115
Step Four, Clancy 50
Step Four from the Big Book 52
Step Four, My homegrown 54
STEPS
  Step One 16–20
  Step Two 20–32
  Step Three 33–44
  Step Four 46–56
  Step Five 55–60
  Step Six 62–76
  Step Seven 76
  Step Eight 82–86
  Step Nine 87–92
  Step Ten 95–108
  Step Twelve 119–128
Step Three decision 35
St. Francis Peace Prayer 141
SUMMARIES
  Summarizing Step One 20
  Summarizing Step Two 32
  Summarizing Step Three 40
  Summarizing Step Four 55–56
  Summarizing Step Five 60–61
  Summarizing Step Six 75
  Summarizing Step Seven 80

Summarizing Step Eight 86
Summarizing Step Nine 91–92
Summarizing Step Ten 107–108
Summarizing Step Eleven 118
Summarizing Step Twelve 127

T

Third Step Prayer 48, 48–49, 49, 125
three As 15
Twelve Steps. See individual Steps
Twelve Step Waltz 6, 15

U

ugly facts 5–6
Understanding 130
unmanageable 16

W

What happened 11–12
What it's like now 13–14
What it was like 6–9
willing to make amends 82, 85, 86
wrongs 55–59, 70, 83, 98, 109

Bird Feet and the Twelve Steps

Acknowledgments

Books do not appear without help and this one has benefited from the help of many wonderful people.

I would like first to thank my "friendly readers" for their invaluable help in making a draft of a book into something worthwhile. Thanks especially to Jennifer Hasenyager and Jill and Steve Hungsburg for their careful reading and their thoughtful, stern suggestions.

Thanks to the many Al-Anons and A.A.s who are the community in which experience has shaped my recovery and this book.

Thanks to my family for their patience while I've growled and grumped my way through the writing.

Thanks especially to my Higher Power for the care that has made my life worth living.

"Bird Feet in Concrete is the best book of its type I've ever used."

"Very helpful throughout my process of recovery."

"Once through won't be enough. This book will reward years of use. Highly recommended."

"Best new 12 Step daily reader in twenty years."

"His candor and honesty gave the words a great deal of weight, giving me new ideas on how to best walk my personal path."

Two meditation books to help you put Twelve-Step wisdom to work in your life every day.

- **Bird Feet In Concrete**:*366 daily meditations for thoughtful Twelve Step seekers*
- **Daily Thoughts and Meditations**: *Steps on the path to recovery*

Two daily meditation books for recovering codependent women and men who seek the good life promised in the Twelve Steps.

Both books thoughtfully weave science, philosophy, religion, and Twelve-Step lore together with the author's personal experiences and quirky observations. The results are engaging, thought-provoking commentaries that range from inspiring to heartbreaking to comic.

Give yourself a quiet moment's peace, some spiritual light to shine on your life, and a moment of inspiration.

Give yourself a daily pause for self-examination, a new idea, or a compassionate message.

Recovery, the journey from chaos to a good life, requires action and a daily dose of clear thinking motivates you and helps you choose actions that take you toward health. These daily readings are vitamins for the mind and soul.

Each book has 366 short meditations full of humanity, insight, and humor.

Bird Feet and the Twelve Steps

www.ingramcontent.com/pod-product-compliance
Lightning Source LLC
LaVergne TN
LVHW051602070426
835507LV00021B/2718